THE UNIVERSITY COLLEGE OF
~~RIPON~~ AND YORK ST. JOHN
YORK CAMPUS

Please return this book by the date stamped below
- if recalled, the loan is reduced to 10 days

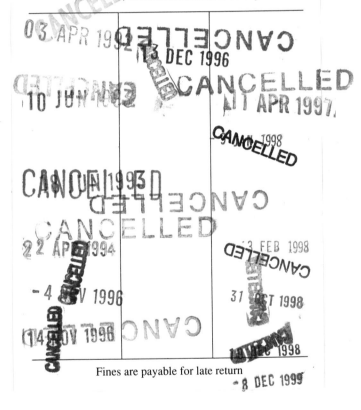

03 APR 1992

13 DEC 1996

CANCELLED

10 JUN

CANCELLED

11 APR 1997

1998

CANCELLED

CANCELLED

JAN 1993

22 APR 1994

3 FEB 1998

-4 NOV 1996

31 OCT 1998

14 NOV 1996

1998

Fines are payable for late return

-8 DEC 1999

A Reader's Guide to
Edwardian Literature

A Reader's Guide to Edwardian Literature

Anthea Trodd
Lecturer in English, University of Keele

Harvester Wheatsheaf

New York   London   Toronto   Sydney   Tokyo   Singapore

First published 1991 by
Harvester Wheatsheaf,
66 Wood Lane End, Hemel Hempstead,
Hertfordshire, HP2 4RG
A division of
Simon & Schuster International Group

Printed and bound in Great Britain by
Billing and Sons Ltd, Worcester

British Library Cataloguing in Publication Data

Trodd, Anthea
  A reader's guide to Edwardian literature.
  1. English literature, 1900–1945 – Critical studies
  I. Title
  820.900912

  ISBN 0-7108-1328-7
  ISBN 0-7108–1336–8 (paperback)

---

1   2   3   4   5   95   94   93   92   91

Contents

Chapter 1

Introduction: Edwardianism

In Virginia Woolf's first novel, *The Voyage Out*, written between 1908 and 1913 and published in 1915, there is a minor character, Miss Allen, who is writing a history of English literature. In Chapter 24 she confides her difficulties with her task to the heroine, Rachel, and to Rachel's fiancé, Terence. ' "Yes, and one has to say something about everybody," Miss Allen added. "That is what I find so difficult, saying something different about everybody." ' This discourages Rachel and Terence; they feel that Miss Allen, engaged in her task of slotting authors into their appropriate places, is placing them too in a long tradition. She 'made them feel that although she would scarcely remember them as individuals, she had laid upon them the burden of the new generation.' [1]

THE LITERARY TRADITION

To Rachel and Terence Miss Allen's activity is appropriate to the older generation. It can also be seen as characteristic of the Edwardian insistence that establishing the tradition of English literature was a major contribution to the assertion of national dignity. Texts and institutions developing that contribution proliferated, affirming the continuity and cultural distinctiveness of English life. Miss Allen's book is presumably intended for the schoolchildren at the lower end of the market. At the upper end the volumes of the *Cambridge History of English Literature* appeared between 1907–16. The *Oxford Book of English Verse* first appeared in 1900, moving the major Victorian anthology, *The Golden Treasury*, into second place. Thomas Hardy's remark that 'his only ambition, so far as he could remember, was to have some poem or poems in a good anthology like the *Golden Treasury*' [2] is suggestive of a new kind of literary consciousness. Keats had speculated 'I think I shall be among the English poets at the time of my death',[3] but Hardy's remark suggests a more precisely formulated idea of how this placing was recognised.

Among the histories of English literature of the period, one was particularly suggestive about the kind of tradition contemplated. Ernest Baker's *History in Fiction*, 1908, was a comprehensive survey of historical fiction, listed in the order of the period setting of each novel, from the Neolithic to the nineteenth century. The volume was international in scope; when English history was completed, sections followed on America, Europe, Africa, Asia and Australasia in that (significant) order. It was intended as a companion to Baker's *Guide to the Best Fiction*, 1903, and sought to demonstrate how novelists had imaginatively recreated every period of the country's history. Baker's earlier guide had many successors. *History and Fiction*, with its assertion of the paramount importance of historical fiction, was characteristic of the Edwardian period, and it is difficult to imagine its publication later.

Two publishing ventures launched in this period offered clear outlines of a canon of English literature to a wide audience. The World's Classics series, founded in 1901 and taken over by Oxford University Press in 1905, and the Everyman's Library, launched by Dent in 1906, defined the works they published as classics to the new reading generation. The *Times Literary Supplement* first appeared in 1902, providing a journal in which the claims of particular works to status within the tradition could be assessed. In 1907 the English Association was established to explain and promote the essential role played by the study of English in the national culture.

The Victorian debate about the desirability of a British equivalent of the Académie Française continued, and culminated in 1910 in the founding of the Academic Committee, a group of writers intended to assert and formalise the dignity and importance of English literature. The twenty-seven founding members included Joseph Conrad, Thomas Hardy, Henry James and W. B. Yeats, as well as Establishment literati of less lasting fame.[4] In the international context, Rudyard Kipling in 1907 became the first English winner of the Nobel Prize for Literature, founded 1901.

In educational institutions this period saw an increasing emphasis on the centrality of the study of English literature, and, in the universities, on the value of English as an academic discipline for ruling-class males, rather than a soft cultural option permissible for female students. The Education Act of 1902, which offered greater opportunities to the lower middle classes to educate their children beyond elementary level, also contributed to the sense that it was important to disseminate a wide awareness of the national heritage. The study of English literature was to be the instrument inculcating a sense of community and tradition in the new state grammar schools. In this period of British hegemony the Romantic concept of literature as expressive of the inner spirit of a nation acquired a new gloss. As English literature was a major part of the supreme national heritage, it was important to establish a precise tradition, and to assert its continuity.[5]

The Edwardian period saw great creativity in what has been called 'the invention of tradition'. Amidst the mass production of traditions in many areas, invention was nowhere more successful than in the ceremonies accumulating around the British monarchy. These intricately stage-managed ceremonies, offering instant tradition as the product of immemorial ages, ran from Victoria's Diamond Jubilee in 1897 to George V's Delhi Durbar in 1911.[6] In the year of the Durbar Ford Madox Ford, one of the most innovative writers and editors of the period, regretted that contemporary poetry was not providing symbols as forceful and popular as those of the ceremonies accumulating around the Crown.[7] It was to this general assertion of imperial dignity that English literature was required to make its contribution. Woolf's Miss Allen, a minor practitioner in the field, is part of this assertion as she writes her history of English literature on the edge of an alien (South American) continent, at the mouth of a great river which has its source deep in the interior, in a heart of darkness, far from civilisation.

In *The Voyage Out* both the young people feel oppressed by Miss Allen's attempt to place them in a tradition. In Terence's case his resistance is couched in terms of his writing ambitions. He has two ideas for novels; the more experimental is for 'a novel about Silence . . . the things people don't say' (Ch. 16). His other proposal, which he outlines in greater detail to Rachel, appears to be a pastiche of a Victorian novel, indebted to Thackeray and Meredith. These two rival possibilities were considered by Woolf herself at the outset of her career. The experimental idea, the novel about silence, Terence finds almost impossible to formulate. The other possibility shows the great Victorian realist tradition exhausted, played out in pastiche, but still exerting a stifling influence over the young writers of the next age.

The problem suggested, of resisting past tradition and locating a modern identity, is a necessary complication to recognise in the Edwardian assertion of continuity and tradition. If tradition was a dominant theme, so too was the assertion of a new, twentieth-century identity. The particular dating of the new age varied. Woolf herself famously placed it in 1910; 'in or about December, 1910, human character changed.' [8] W. B. Yeats, in his introduction to the *Oxford Book of Modern Verse*, remembered a sudden metamorphosis in 1900.[9] These exercises in dating satirise the writing of literary traditions, but still insist strongly that the moderns successfully escaped from Victorianism.

This insistence, an anxiety to define a difference from the Victorians, is dominant among the writers of the period. It was repeated in the next decade when the Georgian poets claimed the new reign in their first anthology, *Georgian Poetry 1911–1912*, even if a number of the poems, as Edward Thomas drily pointed out, were, strictly speaking, Edwardian.[10] The frontier between Victorianism and the twentieth century was variously defined. Arnold Bennett, used by Woolf as her prime example of the patriarchal realist novelist of an outmoded age, had himself little favourable to say about his Victorian predecessors, and attacked the academic critics of the newly dignified discipline of English literature as 'Albert Memorials of learning'.[11]

There were two major new journals committed to the publication of modern writing. The Fabian-backed *New Age*, relaunched in 1907, in which Bennett wrote a regular literary column under the name 'Jacob Tonson', was, despite its socialist mandate and commitment to modern writing, eclectic in its selection of contributors and material. Its more glittering rival, *The English Review*, founded in 1908, was equally eclectic, including among its contributions the first published work of D. H. Lawrence and early poems by Ezra Pound, as well as the work of established figures such as Hardy, James, Conrad and Wells. The two groups were known respectively as the '*Jeunes*' and the '*Immortals*'. Ford Madox Ford, the first editor of *The English Review*, claimed that the journal's title itself was satirically intended:

> It was Conrad who chose the title. He felt a certain sardonic pleasure in the choosing so national a name for a periodical that promised to be singularly international in tone, that was started mainly in his not very English interest and conducted by myself who was growing every day more and more alien to the normal English trend of thought, at any rate in matters of literary technique. And it was matters of literary technique that almost exclusively interested both him and me. That was very unEnglish.[12]

The readership of *The English Review*, however, were not privy to the irony, and the obvious appeal of the name, combined with Ford's professions of unEnglishness, are suggestive of the divided allegiances of this period, not only between traditional and modern, but between national and international.

THE CONTEXT OF MANLINESS

The relation of women writers to the existing tradition was even more problematical than that of the men. In *The Voyage Out* it is Terence, not Rachel, who is struggling with the problem, which was also Woolf's, of how as a writer to resist the existing tradition of literature. Rachel's rejection of tradition is far more comprehensive; by dying at the end of the novel she refuses 'the burden of the new generation', and completely disrupts Miss Allen's orderly tradition.

Woolf's own protracted difficulties in writing this first novel, and her breakdown in 1913 when she concluded it, are matched by her heroine's complete failure to find any place for herself in the society she is entering.[13]

The Edwardian insistence on the identification of literature with the national and imperial spirit, and the accumulation of institutions and forms of writing expressing that identification, meant that literature was increasingly seen in a masculine context. This was a period when the voice of the masculine ruling class was particularly dominant in the culture. Raymond Williams suggests that there was a crucial shift in the late nineteenth century when

> the vision of Englishness itself changes; whereas earlier it is really internal to England, in the 1880–1920 period it is far more defined in terms of an external imperial role. . . . From now on what it was to be English was quite new. It was defined in very insulated ways, within these very hard trainings, within increasingly standardised and masculine institutions.[14]

In the earlier nineteenth century the novel was still seen as a field appropriate enough to the untrained female writer, but with the rise in status of the novel, and the increasing professionalisation of the novelist, this changed. N. N. Feltes, in his *Modes of Production of Victorian Novels*, argues that the professional organisation of novel-writing redefined it as a masculine activity.[15] In 1911 the Academic Committee confirmed this identification of the professional and the masculine by its exclusion policies, described by Samuel Hynes in *Edwardian Occasions*. The first two proposed members to be blackballed were the novelist May Sinclair and the male, but Indian, Rabindranath Tagore (proposed by Yeats). Tagore was excluded as a foreigner, albeit from within the Empire; the institutionalising of the dignity of literature defined it as white and male.[16]

Evidence that members of the Committee regarded their exclusive group as 'literature' was provided by Henry James's reaction to H. G. Wells's refusal to join. When Wells stated his objection to 'hierarchies', James wrote to a fellow member that Wells had 'cut loose from literature clearly–practically altogether'.[17] Literature thus was defined as a particular and exclusive group. (After much publicity the Academic Committee did admit a woman, Lady

Ritchie, who, as a titled septuagenarian and Thackeray's daughter, was probably the least threatening possibility to be found.)

Women and foreigners were identified by the Academic Committee as the excluded. In the Edwardian period Englishness was closely associated with masculinity, and 'manliness' was seen as a dominant characteristic of English literature. The consensus of the Edwardian literary hierarchy that theirs was an exceptionally masculine age persists. Three-quarters of a century later, it was reiterated in a memoir by Isaiah Berlin, who describes them:

> the Edwardians – full-blooded, masculine men of letters, with sometimes coarse (and even to some degree philistine) but vital personalities . . . [their] talk was hearty, concerned with royalties, publishers, love affairs, absurd adventures, society scandals, and anecdotes about famous persons, accompanied by gusts of laughter, puns, limericks, a great deal of mutual banter, jokes about women, money and foreigners, and with a great deal of drink. The atmosphere was that of a male dining club of vigorous, amusing, sometimes rather vulgar friends.[18]

There are discrepancies. Wells, who consciously defined himself as philistine, refused to be grouped; James, who was an enthusiastic advocate of grouping, hardly conformed to Berlin's picture. The description, however, does emphasise the self-consciously masculine identity of the profession of letters in the Edwardian period.

In 1894 Kipling, the writer most closely associated with the masculine imperial ethos, wrote a poem, 'The Three-Decker', to mark the end of the dominance of the three-volume novel, hitherto the preferred form of the circulating libraries, and therefore the form in which most novels were first published. In the poem the three-decker is figured as a sailing-ship which sails off into the sunset, taking with her the world of the old-fashioned novel, with its narratives by nurses, its happy endings, its moral certainties. She is replaced by steamships, sophisticated, technological and definitely masculine. The poem presents itself as an affectionate tribute:

> Her crews are babes or madmen? Her port is all to make?
> You're manned by Truth and Science, and you steam for steaming's sake?
> Well – tinker up your engines – you know your business best,
> *She's* taking tired people to the Islands of the Blest.[19]

The suggestion is of a now outmoded world of old-fashioned fictions for women and children and those too tired for anything but light reading, which has yielded to a new world of consciously artistic fictions produced by men for men. The irony directed at the latter was characteristic of Kipling, who, like Wells, avoided literary groups.

This suggested opposition of male and female fictions became one way of defining the relation of the new age with that of Victoria. The revolt against Victorianism was to a large extent couched in terms of a revolt against an over-feminised literature. An analogy was provided by the two monarchs; literary Victorianism, like the Queen, had lingered on too long and obstructed her virile heir. The tendency to characterise Victorian literature as innately feminine was widespread. Henry James, in an essay of 1902, urged the value of Flaubert to English novelists as lying in his mastery of form and composition. These considerations have been missing from the English novel 'because the novel is so preponderantly cultivated among us by women, in other words by a sex ever gracefully, comfortably, enviably unconscious (it would be too much to call them even suspicious) of the requirements of form.' [20] The alleged dominance of the woman writer had held the English novel back from realising the formal perfections of the great European works.

The literary equivalent of Victoria was George Eliot, whose reputation at this point was at its lowest ebb, even allowing for the general slump in Victorian reputations. In the new *Cambridge History of English Literature*, her novels were discussed alongside the documentary fictions of Kingsley and Disraeli. A slimmer volume of assessment, G. K. Chesterton's *The Victorian Age in Literature*, 1913, attributed Victorian bowdlerism to 'the participation of women with men in the matter of fiction . . . the sexes can only be coarse apart', and went on to discuss 'the general moral atmosphere in the Victorian age . . . everyone will understand me if I call it George Eliot'. [21]

Arnold Bennett persistently referred to her in his writings as the type of a fussy, artless Victorianism. 'She was too preoccupied by moral questions to be a first-class creative artist. And she was a woman', [22] he declared, and later, 'artistic ambition overweened in the unhappy lady and she wrote *Middlemarch*'.[23] Rereading Dickens, he was aghast to find that the greatest male writer of the Victorian age had been contaminated by such feminine artlessness, and he expressed his horror in scathing masculine slang; 'of all the rotten, vulgar, unliterary writing . . . worse than George Eliot's. If a novelist can't *write*, where *is* the beggar?'[24]

The academic defenders of English literature, asserting the new prestige of a discipline once seen as a lower form of cultivation for female students, were equally urgent on the equation of literature with masculinity. At Cambridge Sir Arthur Quiller-Couch, the King Edward VII Professor of English Literature, was advising his students to look for style in 'the great, masculine, objective writers', and assuring them that 'the more of catholic mankind you inherit from those great loins the more you will assuredly beget'.[25] Clearly there was little place for female readers, let alone writers, in this patriarchal tradition. Quiller-Couch's colleague, Professor Sir Walter Raleigh, who in 1904 became the first holder of the Chair of English Literature at Oxford, took a more dangerously provocative line in manliness. Woolf was to pounce delightedly on this aptly named Professor's buccaneering confession 'I can't help feeling that critical admiration for what another man has written is an emotion for spinsters.'[26]

Raleigh's reckless comment exposes the defensiveness of English literature at the time, asserting its newly virile status after an age of supposed female dominance. He also undermined its pretensions; if reading was an activity suitable only for celibate females, where were the claims of English literature to express the spirit of imperial Britain? Sandra Gilbert and Susan Gubar have argued in their analysis of gender politics in twentieth-century writing, *No Man's Land*, 1988-9, that much modernist writing has its roots in the reaction against the rise of feminist consciousness and organisation.[27] It is certainly true that this last, immediately pre-modernist period was marked by an assertive but highly defensive masculinity in writing, while the political activities of the suffragettes were not matched by any strong female presence in literature.

The 1890s had seen a wave of writing, by male and female writers, on the subject of the New Woman, but this had declined by the new century. During the Edwardian period Woolf was writing her first novel and experiencing great difficulties, which may be partly explained by the climate of the time. Towards the end of the period Katherine Mansfield's short stories began appearing, and Dorothy Richardson produced the first volume of her 'stream of consciousness' novel, *Pilgrimage*. Elizabeth Robins's suffragette novel, *The Convert*, 1907, and Olive Schreiner's study, *Women and Labour*, 1911, were leading examples of women's polemic of the period. These contributions to mainstream writing were not enough to impinge on the 'men's club' image of literary activity.

Where women were visible was in genres of lower status. If one were to name the most enduringly known work published by a woman in this period, it would probably have to be Baroness Orczy's *The Scarlet Pimpernel*, 1905, with its nearest competitor as Frances Hodgson Burnett's *The Secret Garden*, 1911. The immediate success of Orczy, a Hungarian, in creating a popular archetype of English chauvinism, who asserted his national superiority by obstructing the revolutionary activities of another country, clearly identifies her as a female writer very close to the Edwardian national consciousness. Burnett's book, written specifically for juvenile female readers, was also conservative and aristocratic in sympathies. Women were prominent in the genres of popular romance and children's literature. The most consistent producer of children's classics in the period was Edith Nesbit. The romance market was dominated by Marie Corelli, who carried her mass readership forward into the new century, and by other women romancers such as Florence Barclay, Ethel M. Dell and Elinor Glyn.

THE SEARCH FOR AN AUDIENCE

Corelli's audience far exceeded that of any of the critically regarded writers of the period. Her 1895 bestseller, *The Sorrows of Satan*, carried a triumphant note announcing that no review copies had been sent out; the author was addressing the public directly. Such success contributed to the picture of a reading public divided between a cultured masculine élite and a mass readership predominantly female and catered for by females.

In 1895 James summarised this in a short story, 'The Next Time', in which a best-selling female novelist attempts to produce something of aesthetic value that will be beyond her mass readership, while her brother-in-law, a genius recognised by a small, discriminating public, tries to prostitute himself to a mass audience. She, despite her feminine incapacity for form, searches for his 'secret', and he for hers, though, significantly, it is his wife whom he sends researching for models among the romantic fiction in the libraries, 'foraging further afield for him than he could conveniently go'.[28] Neither finds the other's secret. Both continue to be successful in their particular line as best seller or unread genius, and part of the explanation is clearly the secret of gender.

James's story anticipated modernism's rejection of those aesthetic forms, such as the realistic novel, associated with Victorianism and with commercialised mass culture, and he offered a gendered reading of this rejection. The story is also an ironic comment on his own futile search for an audience in the face of what he registered as an absolute contradiction between the serious novel and the best seller.

This sense of contradiction, of bafflement at the increasing development of mass culture, and the proliferation of specialised reading publics, is endemic in the period. Peter Keating points out, in his *The Haunted Study*, that this was a belated awakening to the long-standing existence of a larger reading public, which mid-Victorian cultural assumptions about a unified market had contrived to disregard.[29] The writers of the turn of the century, facing a reading public continually expanding and fragmenting into specialised audiences, were forced to register these hitherto ignored changes.

Edwardian writers were continually speculating about the nature of the audience they addressed. Bennett worried at the subject in his *New Age* columns; 'it is well for novelists to remember . . . that their professional existence depends on the fact that the dullest class in England takes to novels merely as a refuge from its own dullness.'[30] Bennett was gloomily contemplating his middle-class readership.

Wells's apprehensions took a different form. 'It is scarcely too much to say that every writer of our time who can be called popular owes three-quarters of his or her fame to the girls who have been taught in board-school.' [31] Later in the period he cheered up; 'among readers, women and girls and young men at least will insist upon having their novels significant and real'. [32]

James's bafflement at 'the broad-backed public . . . which, consistently and consummately unable to give the smallest account of itself, naturally renders no grain of help to enquiry' [33] is echoed throughout the period. In some works, for instance Conrad's *Heart of Darkness* and Ford's *The Good Soldier*, the search for an audience becomes part of the narrative process. Even the most innovative writers in fiction had not abandoned the hope of a popular audience. James satirised his own search in 'The Next Time'. Conrad was the type of the serious experimental writer read by a small, discriminating audience, but he worked persistently in popular forms.

Edward VII reigned from 1901 to 1910. I have extended the scope of this book to the outbreak of World War I in 1914. Woolf placed the arrival of a new age in 1910; many writers have treated the period 1870 or 1880 to 1914 as homogenous in its reaction against high Victorianism. Edward's accession, however, coinciding with the new century, did represent to many writers a possibility for confident assertion of a complete break from Victorianism, and for formulating the identity of the new age.

Some writers produced most of their major work in this period, including Conrad, Forster and Wells. For others, Hardy, James, Yeats, it was one phase in a long career. Many of the new writers associated with modernism published their first works in this period. These works belong to the history of modernism, but their part in the Edwardian debate about the rejection of Victorian forms and beliefs requires some mention. The particular rejection expressed in the work of the women writers who began publishing towards the end of the period requires more extensive attention; it offers some explanation for the marginality of women's writing in this period.

The attempt to define Englishness and the English tradition was a

central part of Edwardianism. Bennett and Woolf, frequent antagonists, coincided in their belief that, at this moment of crisis for
English fiction, it was not very helpful that a Pole should be at the
helm. Woolf commented that 'Mr Conrad is a Pole; which sets him
apart, and makes him, however admirable, not very useful.' [34]
Conrad, in fact, had much to say about Englishness, and his
commentary is used in the next chapter as the entry into Edwardianism. On the other hand, Pound and Joyce related to an internationalist and modernist tradition, though they published their
first works in this period.

A related point is the use of the words 'English' and 'British'.
Then as now people speaking about national identity slid easily and
confusingly from one to the other. Britain suggested geography and
the Empire, England a non-political entity which included the shires,
(but not the provinces), and their immemorial ways. The Aliens Act
of 1905 obstructed the passage of immigrants into Britain, but it was
'England' its supporters claimed to be defending. I have attempted
to observe this distinction by referring to 'England', except where
the immediate context, geographical or legal, demands 'Britain'.

Chapters 2 and 3 describe the Edwardian concern with national
identity. Chapter 2 looks at the literature of imperialism, the
dominant ideology of the period, at the search for narrative forms to
explore the psychological significance of imperialism, and the
anticipation of later debates about the post-imperialist crisis of
national identity. Chapter 3 discusses the attempts to describe an
alternative, non-imperial, 'English' identity, which drew on the
methods of the Victorian social panoramic novel, and on the
imagery of rural life, to conduct a debate about which groups were
to be considered representatively 'English'.

Chapter 4 examines the theme of generational revolt popular in
works of the period, and the accompanying rejection of literary
forms, especially the realist novel, associated with Victorianism.
These reactions were part of the transition to modernism. Chapter 5
discusses women's reactions against tradition, the attempts of male
writers to understand these reactions, and the entry of women
writers into the debate late in the period.

Chapter 6 looks at the poetry of the period, at the ideals of

Impressionism, and at poets' share in the Edwardian search for an identifiable audience. Chapter 7 examines contemporary debates about the future of the novel, centering on the James–Wells debate where James argued for the central role of formal experiment in the novel, and Wells for the novel as a popular medium for discussion of political issues, and of the psychological problems raised by social change. This debate summarised the sense of crisis in literature endemic at the period. The English writer was anxious to re-examine his relation with the literary tradition and to formulate a new identity. The following chapters describe the diversity of that debate.

Chapter 2

The imperial identity

In 1896 H. G. Wells, reviewing the latest imperialist romance by Rider Haggard, regretted the genre's popularity with boys because 'it must fill their heads with very silly ideas about the invulnerability and other privileges of the Englishman abroad'.[1] Imperialist fiction, as Wells suggested, purveyed a particular idea of the Englishman as self-contained, unexcitable, impervious to outside influence, his apartness from inferior races guaranteed. It was this idea Conrad invoked when he enquired into the imperialist character of his adopted race in his great novel of imperial adventurism in South America, *Nostromo*, 1904. The racially typical imperturbability of Charles Gould, the major English character, is discussed by two of his compatriots. The engineer, new to the country, says 'That man is calmness itself. . . . He must be extremely sure of himself.' The doctor, who has experienced under torture the limits of English invulnerability, replies 'If that's all he's sure of, then he is sure of nothing. . . . It is the last thing a man ought to be sure of.'[2]

FICTION AND EMPIRE

Imperialism was the dominant national ideology of the Edwardian period. The imperialist romances promoted an idea of the Englishman which emerged from the ruling-class cult of masculinity established in the public schools since the middle of the nineteenth century. The school stories popular during this period charted a shift from Christian manliness to a distinct imperialist emphasis.[3] Kipling's *Stalky & Co.*, 1899, which described a public school training ground for the future defenders of empire, showed the boys as rebellious to the masters, resistant to emotional appeals and continually derisive of the goody-goody heroes of previous school classics. The independent manliness Stalky and his friends learned fitted them for the frontiers of empire.

To be manly was to be impervious to the emotionalism and excitability of those defined as inferior by race. This idea evolved from the needs of a ruling class to whom the imperial experience introduced ideas of cultural relativism, and who were anxious to justify English hegemony with concepts of English racial and moral superiority. However, manliness did not simply require exclusion of inferior qualities. The nineteenth century developed a science of racialism, and in fiction this was represented by the frequent requirement that the hero show knowledge of, even empathy with, his inferiors. Anything they could do, he could do, or at least understand, better. His just claims to hegemony were supported by his accumulated knowledge, his 'scientific' understanding of the dominated.[4]

The imperial character was originally that of the ruling-class male, who defined himself as superior to other races in terms comparable to those in which he defined his superiority to those of inferior class or gender. The interchangeability of the language and imagery of race, class and gender is continually demonstrated in the texts of this period. The popular imperialist romances, however, made imperial masculinity available to a much wider male readership. The late nineteenth century saw a steep rise in boys' fiction, and in adventure stories directed at the male reader which promoted the imperial adventurer as hero.[5] The proliferation of periodicals for a new mass readership in the last twenty years of the nineteenth century included many boys' journals following on the success of *The Boys' Own Paper*, founded in 1879. The Edwardian successes in boys' periodicals were *The Magnet* and *The Gem*, and the secure world picture they promoted was memorably celebrated by George Orwell in the article 'Boys' weeklies':

The King is on his throne and the pound is worth a pound. Over in Europe the comic foreigners are jabbering and gesticulating, but the grim grey battleships of the British Fleet are steaming up the Channel and at the outposts of Empire the monocled Englishmen are holding the niggers at bay.[6]

Such fictions, and the imperialist bias of much of the press and of the music-hall, offered the English male outside the ruling class an opportunity to imagine his participation in the superiority of the English imperialist. As Eric Hobsbawm says in *The Age of Empire*:

imperialism encouraged the masses, and especially the potentially discontented, to identify themselves with the imperial state and nation, and thus unconsciously to endow the social and political system represented by that state with justification and legitimacy . . . empire made good ideological cement.[7]

In the great pro-imperialist Edwardian novel, Kipling's *Kim*, 1901, that most winning summons to the colours, the juvenile hero's origins are Irish and Catholic and working-class. Kipling's argument for a permanent Raj required the incorporation of such potential imperialist material, though this degree of inclusiveness was not advocated by all writers.

The major Victorian novels were directed to a family audience, even if the novelists often lamented the restrictions this audience imposed. Some commentators saw an important departure for fiction in the emergence in the late nineteenth century, amid the growing specialisation of audiences for fiction and journals, of the romance addressed to a male readership. Romance was the term applied to fiction which employed the exotic, adventurous or fantastic, as opposed to the ordinary life described by realism. The positive response to romance was formulated by the critic Andrew Lang, in an 1887 article 'Realism and romance'. Lang hailed the new wave of romances as a welcome corrective to the tired genre of Victorian realism.

The strength of the romance for Lang lay in its recognition of 'our mixed condition, civilised at the top with the old barbarian under our clothes'. Its appeal was distinctively macho, to 'the natural man within me, the survival of some blue-painted Briton or of some gipsy'. In contrast 'any clever man or woman may elaborate a realistic novel according to the rules'. While the principal living exponent of this cleverness seemed to be Henry James, realism was seen as primarily associated with the late George Eliot and with 'the microscopic examination of the hearts of young girls'.[8] Lang offered a gendered interpretation of genres in which the new masculine romance superseded feminine realism. His frequent references to *Huckleberry Finn* evoked an impression of male readers of the period as so many Huck Finns, longing to light out for new territories and escape Aunt Sally. His scenario of a male backlash against a feminised mainstream tradition has received some critical support in recent years.[9]

Ten years later George Gissing, himself working well within the tradition of the realist novel, allowed the hero of his novel, *The Whirlpool*, to respond enthusiastically to Kipling's appeal to the 'millions of men, natural men, revolting against the softness and sweetness of civilisation'.[10] *The Whirlpool* portrayed an England dangerously feminised and decadent, and imagined a possible revolt towards manliness in a literature addressed specifically to male readers.

Around the turn of the century the ceremonials of empire accumulated, inviting mass participation in the idea of empire. It was also a time when events enforced reassessment of the English imperial character. The Boer War, with its early military failures, its controversial policies, including the pioneering of concentration camps and its provocation of jingoistic mass disorder, or mafficking, on the streets of Britain, called into question accepted notions of that character. Britain's claim to moral superiority was lost on a Europe largely sympathetic to the Boers. Writers from the right and the left urged a rethinking of the imperial role in the name of 'national efficiency', the popular political slogan of the time.[11] Kipling assessed the dangers in the poems 'The Islanders' and 'The Lesson', 1902; 'We have had no end of a lesson, it will do us no end of good'.[12] Shaw, in the pamphlet *Fabianism and Empire*, 1900, urged on socialists the long-term advantages of an imperialist phase.

Another significant marker in the definition of national character came when the Aliens Act of 1905 formalised a new national sense of apartness. The restrictions on immigration introduced to check the influx of refugees, mostly Jewish, from Eastern Europe, announced the end of Britain's traditional image as a haven for fugitives from Continental tyrannies. The original proposals included one to designate particular areas of the East End as British preserves. The minority of Liberal opposition MPs who opposed the Bill regretted the breach in Britain's long traditions of hospitality. One political refugee from Eastern Europe, Joseph Conrad, wrote *The Secret Agent*, 1906, during the months when the Aliens Bill was being debated, and he opposed foreign 'agitators' and English police and politicians in a critical enquiry into the myths of the English character.

Conrad and Kipling were the two major writers to treat imperialist matters in the Edwardian period. They worked within the romance genre, and were often classified as romance writers, though neither would have accepted the classification. Their respective first works of the period, *Heart of Darkness* and *Kim*, share a common theme. In imperialist fictions the reverse of the invulnerable self-contained imperialist hero is the European who goes native. Conrad's Mr Kurtz and Kipling's Kim are variations on this theme.

Both heroes also work for front organisations which assert a civilising scientific influence on colonised countries, Kurtz for the Society for the Suppression of Savage Customs, which is a looters' charter, and Kim for the Ethnographical Survey, which is an arm of the British secret service. Both discover an ability to empathise with, and impersonate, the behaviour of subject races. The two books suggest the unsatisfactoriness of the existing heroic model of imperialist invulnerability, but, where *Kim* asserts that true imperial efficiency lies in the imperialist's ability to master the subject race through empathy and knowledge, Conrad demonstrates the frailty of the idea of superiority and invulnerability on which empire is based.

CONRAD: *HEART OF DARKNESS*

In 1899, when *Heart of Darkness* was serialised in *Blackwood's Magazine*, Conrad was already known as a writer of several romances with colonial or maritime settings. His critical manifesto, the preface to *The Nigger of the Narcissus*, 1897, had also identified him as an artist who worked in the novel as a consciously aesthetic form, and represented the serious future of the novel, (see Chapter 7). He offered *Heart of Darkness* to Blackwood, however, as a documentary, rather than an aesthetic contribution, and one based on his own experiences of imperialism in the Congo in 1890. 'The criminality of inefficiency and pure selfishness when tackling the civilising work in Africa is a justifiable idea. The subject is of our time distinctly – though not topically treated.' [13]

The description is carefully tailored to contemporary requirements, and suggests Conrad's willingness to seek a wider audience than he had hitherto won. National efficiency was a watchword of the period, and was to become even more urgent as the Boer War progressed. The imperialist hero, Kurtz, was European, 'all Europe contributed to the making of Kurtz',[14] but working specifically for Leopold of Belgium, whose savage excesses in his private fief, the Congo, had been the subject of Parliamentary debate since 1897.

Heart of Darkness was written in the months leading up to the outbreak of the Boer War, the first imperialist crisis of the Edwardian period. Conrad, in his letters, expressed fears of the consequences for the national character of the 'ruthless repression' that must attend 'a war which to be effective must be a war of extermination'.[15] This fear was widespread at the period. One influential work of the previous decade, which had countered ideas of racial superiority and the ethos of imperial struggle, was Thomas Huxley's *Evolution and Ethics*, 1894. Huxley had warned of the antagonism between the cosmic process and humanity's ethical aspirations, and had outlined the possibility of an evolutionary regression.[16]

To many liberal commentators the Boer War seemed to be realising the beginnings of that regression. The major liberal critique of imperialism of the period, John Hobson's *Imperialism*, 1902, a critique later adapted and extended by Lenin, warned that the major consequence of empire for Britain would be a barbarisation of the national character. In his earlier *The Psychology of Jingoism*, 1901, he saw the mafficking crowds on the streets and the operations of imperialist media, the jingo press, the music-hall, imperialist fictions for boys, as evidence that the British were regressing to the savagery of those nations they pretended to civilise.

Heart of Darkness, like its immediate successor, *Lord Jim*, 1900, is the story of a European who ceases to be 'one of us'. The situation of Kurtz going native in the Congo focuses the fears which are the dark side of the belief in imperial invulnerability. At the end of his report on what civilisation can do for the inhabitants of the Congo Kurtz scrawls 'Exterminate all the brutes!' One of the most frequent charges brought by the liberal opposition in Britain to the Boer War was the virulent fomenting of anti-Dutch feeling by the British in South Africa in the months leading up to the war. The phrase 'Exterminate the vermin' was repeatedly cited by the pro-Boers as a typical British slogan in South Africa.[17] Kurtz's regression to savagery enacts the fears of those liberals and radicals who saw the entire British nation going native.

Alongside these fears of a regressive mutation in the national character, the colonial experience brought a general exposure to cultural relativism. The experiences in the Congo of the English narrator, Marlow, force on him a realisation of the social construction of personality. As he tells his hearers:

> You can't understand. How could you? – with solid pavement under your feet, surrounded by kind neighbours ready to cheer you or to fall on you, stepping delicately between the butcher and the policeman, in the holy terror of scandal and gallows and lunatic asylums – how can you imagine what particular regions of the first ages a man's untrammelled feet may take him into by the way of solitude – utter solitude without a policeman. (Ch. 2)

The theme of going native was one expression of the general breakdown of the concept of stable, knowable, coherent identity, what D. H. Lawrence called 'the old stable ego',[18] which informed the classic realism of the nineteenth century. The alteration of his frame of reference makes it impossible for Marlow to 'know' himself or Kurtz, or to assist his hearers to the position of enlightened overseers of his narrative.

Before Marlow leaves Brussels for the Congo he is examined by the Company doctor, who takes a scientific interest in the personality changes which affect the Company's men in the Congo. 'You are the first Englishman coming under my observation' (Ch. 1). It is Kurtz's disintegration which we observe, but his English colleague loses his own assumptions about the 'old stable ego'. Conrad's later works in the decade emphasise how the imperial context invalidates the concept of the stable ego. In *Lord Jim* Marlow's attempts to confirm the grounds on which Jim is 'one of us' are continually baffled.[19]

The use of journeys in 'the dark places of the earth' (Ch. 1) as journeys of psychological self-discovery had been common in European literature in the nineteenth century. Edward Said's *Orientalism* demonstrates the use of the East as the dark Other against which the Westerner defined himself.[20] In the theme of going native, however, the implied threat is that there might be no difference to discover; in *Heart of Darkness* that threat is realised.

The realisation of this threat, however, is in continually contradictory relation with the romance form. *Blackwood's Magazine* addressed itself to a professional, middle-class audience, and had recently published a number of romances of male adventure.[21] It offered Conrad an established context for the telling of imperial fictions, and for the *Blackwood's* audience he evolved an appropriate narrative persona, the English master mariner, Charlie Marlow. Marlow, who was to be kept in regular work in later writings from *Lord Jim* on, allowed Conrad to assume an easier and more direct relation with his readers than before. His earlier working of his Congo experiences, the short story 'An Outpost of Progress', 1898, had recorded the criminality of imperialism through an omniscient and invisible narrator. In *Heart of Darkness* the narrative of imperialism is told within an English context.

Marlow's audience is made up of male professionals, like the audiences within many of Kipling's stories, or that in Wells's *The Time Machine*, 1895, to which *Heart of Darkness* bears a strong structural similarity. The shared references between Marlow and his audience are English. Marlow's tale is a narrative of imperial adventurism told to a male professional audience within the tale by a sea dog who invokes the names of Drake and Franklin. This audience duplicates *Blackwood's Magazine*'s male professional readership as Marlow duplicates ex-master mariner Conrad. This arrangement may suggest the complicity of English imperialism in the Belgian-administered atrocities in the Congo, but it also suggests a hankering after the lost intimacy and security of the story-teller with an assured audience.

Heart of Darkness evoked a particular solidarity, the solidarity suggested by *Blackwood's* guaranteed audience of professional males concerned with issues of imperial management and destiny. The narrative, however, questions if this audience can be reached. The search for an audience becomes increasingly explicit within the text. Marlow continually doubts his ability to communicate; the frame narrator suspects his co-listeners have fallen asleep. Darkness engulfs the search for meaning, and the assertion of solidarity.

In a 1905 essay on Henry James, a writer with a notably limited readership, Conrad suggested that the artist's pursuit of his meaning long outlasts his audience's willingness to listen. He envisaged a Last Day when the artist will continue to tell stories but 'I doubt the heroism of the hearers'.[22] *Heart of Darkness* enacts this Last Day, clinging to the possibility of a known audience, while still doubting its capacity to follow the teller.

If the attention of Marlow's male listeners is doubtful, there is another audience which is formally excluded. The audience, as for other romances, is emphatically masculine, and in this case we are continually reminded that the story is untellable to women. Early in his narrative Marlow muses 'It's queer how out of touch with truth women are' (Ch. 1), and he later reveals that he entirely failed to tell his story to the woman most closely concerned, Kurtz's Intended. 'I could not tell her. It would have been too dark – too dark altogether' (Ch. 3).

Marlow's failure affirms the gender polarity round which imperialism is formed. The significantly titled Intended was the major motive for Kurtz's journey, and represented to him the civilising ideals he wished to fulfil in his conquest of Africa. She is the major topic of his conversation, 'my Intended, my ivory, my station, my river', and therefore, when Marlow tells her that Kurtz's last words were her name, he is perhaps offering a reasonable paraphrase of 'The horror! The horror!'

The idealistic Intended is duplicated in the painting by Kurtz of a blindfolded woman carrying a torch, which Marlow sees in the trading-station. In the conventional racist dualism of the nineteenth century the purity of the white woman was the emblem of moral and racial superiority, and its defence the justification of imperialism. Kurtz's African mistress represented the feared and therefore excluded female sexuality. But in becoming the emblem and justification of imperialism, European women could also sometimes be identified as the cause of imperialist oppression. The presence of the memsahib came to be seen as the principal explanation for imperial severity in India.[23] The well-meaning aunt who gets Marlow his Congo job, and the three knitters in the Brussels office who oversee his departure, are parodic versions of the female idealism which sends Kurtz to his destruction.

The idealism which supports the extermination in the Congo remains untouched. 'Oh, she is out of it - completely. They - the women I mean - are out of it - should be out of it. We must help them to stay in that beautiful world of their own, lest ours gets worse' (Ch. 2). Kurtz's successors will continue to justify the dark masculine 'secret' of imperialism as a preservation of the ideals of their Intendeds. In *Heart of Darkness* the solidarity implicit in the exclusive masculine romance audience becomes the condition which assures the continuation of imperialist atrocities.

CONRAD: LORD JIM, NOSTROMO, THE SECRET AGENT

Conrad's later Edwardian novels conduct a critical enquiry into the specifically English idea of imperialist apartness. *Lord Jim*, 1900, like *Heart of Darkness* serialised in *Blackwood's*, examines the kind of imagination produced by the reading of romances of masculine adventure. Jim's juvenile reading has given him the sense of invulnerability and privilege which Wells feared. The idea of heroic distinctiveness he learns from his reading proves less appropriate to crisis than the workable sense of duty which sustains the French officer who salvages the ship Jim deserts. Jim's failure precipitates self-enquiry among his compatriots, anxious to learn how representative the vulnerability of 'one of us' is. The chairman of the court of enquiry, a type of the reserved and impervious Englishman, commits suicide without comment.

Conrad's narrative rejects not only the hero of romance, but also the realist novel's assumption of stable, continuous identity; Marlow fails to organise a coherent narrative from the varied evidence about Jim he accumulates. The Patusan episode, which treats Jim's attempt to recreate his heroic ideal, does so in the terms of romance, and has proved a continuing critical problem to readers unable to reconcile this episode, 'a virtual paradigm of romance',[24] with the experimental narrative techniques of Marlow's framing investigation. The problem suggests that Conrad was reluctant to choose between the wide audience afforded by romance, and the small audience for innovative fiction.

In *Nostromo*, 1904, the romance paradigm occupies a much more marginal position. This massive construction of the geography and history of Costaguana, a fictional South American republic with some resemblance to Colombia, traces a revolution effected by the money and management skills of an Anglo-American alliance. In a late episode the story of the actual revolutionary coup is told as heroic romance by the only possible narrator, the old sea dog Captain Mitchell, whose perennial boyishness makes him capable of believing in the heroism of deeds of which the reader already has a far more sceptical understanding. He represents the general English reader, to whom such romance is the only acceptable form in which imperialist adventurism can be narrated.

As in *Heart of Darkness*, the role of the female characters is to provide inspiration and justification for the imperialist adventurism from which they are excluded. Antonia is a type of the Intended, last seen urging another coup, which will extend the effects of the previous coup she inspired. Emilia Gould, who is aware of her exclusion from her husband's business world, still provides in her philanthropic activities the acceptable face of his capitalist ventures.

Charles Gould, the manager of the silver mine, is a type of the English imperial hero of the most invulnerable kind. The novel exposes his unresponsiveness both to his wife and to the effects of the revolution he has 'managed', but it also provides another kind of criticism. In this venture of economic imperialism, which uses a popular revolution to acquire effective control over a South American state, the interests of the United States are paramount. The book charts a shift in imperial dominance from English to North American imperial interests. Gould is merely a manager for the latter. *Nostromo* foreshadows a time when the English will have to realise that they are no longer the dominant imperialist power.

A comparable questioning of the English sense of privileged apartness takes place in *The Secret Agent*, 1906. This novel responds to the Aliens Bill debates of 1904–5 in its picture of a complacent London infiltrated by Continental layabouts posing as political refugees, and by *agents provocateurs* from tsarist Russia, that 'ravenous ghoul' described in Conrad's major political essay 'Autocracy and War', 1905.[25] In 1906 Britain had an influx of Russian refugees from the failed revolution of 1905 at a time when it had revised its status as a haven for such refugees.

Conrad questioned both the basis of the traditional liberal idea of Britain as the haven for Europe, and the ability of the English to come to terms with a situation in which they are no longer a race apart. The *agent provocateur* in the Russian embassy, Mr Vladimir, and the anarchist bomb expert, the Professor, are alike in seeking to force the English into an awareness that they are part of a Europe feverish with political intrigue. Chance and their incompetence defeat them this time, but the novel suggests that this respite may be only temporary.

KIPLING: KIM

By 1901 when Kipling produced his most famous romance, *Kim*, he was widely known as the major writer of imperialism through several collections of stories, beginning with *Plain Tales from the Hills*, 1888, and of poems, beginning with *Departmental Ditties*, 1886, and the children's book, *The Jungle Book*, 1894. Wells in *The New Machiavelli*, 1911, placed the height of Kipling's influence in the 1890s, when his hero–narrator records: 'The prevailing force in my undergraduate days was not socialism but Kiplingism.' [26] During the Boer War Conrad sardonically attributed still greater influence to Kipling, suggesting that the British reverses were the result of the Almighty's displeasure at the dubious theology of 'Recessional', 1897, his much admired imperialist hymn. [27]

In *Kim*, a story ostensibly directed to a male juvenile audience, the boy hero has gone native before the story begins, and gradually discovers his identity with British imperial fortunes, and his role in the Great Game of espionage. Like *Heart of Darkness*, *Kim* questions 'the old stable ego', but Kim's ever-extending capacity for empathetic impersonation of different races and creeds celebrates the values of going native. The adult English characters in the novel are narrow and fixed in their imperviousness to their surroundings. Although the school which Kim attends 'looks down on boys who have gone native altogether', [28] the degree to which Kim has preserved a residual sahib identity remains in question for much of the book.

Kim's enjoyment in impersonating other races suggests a genuine reworking of the idea of identity, a celebration of the possibility of escaping the fixed, socially constructed forms of racial identity. As A. R. JanMohammed argues, the 'ability to forgo a permanent fixed self, which is essential if one is going to understand a racial or cultural alterity, is turned into a positive principle in *Kim*.' [29] Kipling tells us Kim's racial identity in the second paragraph of the novel, but we may have difficulty retaining the information as the novel explores the dissolution of a fixed identity resulting from Kim's adoption of a succession of roles. The brotherhood of the Great Game is multiracial; Kim learns that the despised Bengali, Hurree, is 'one of us' (Ch. 9).

The capacity 'to enter another's soul' (Ch. 9) can also, however, be read as a sign of Western superiority; Hurree's considerable talents at role-playing do not extend to impersonating a Westerner. The Indian boy with whom Kim shares his first lessons in espionage lacks Kim's Western ability to resist hypnosis. The gift for successful mimicry of race or class or even gender inferiors was often credited to romance heroes of the period; it was part of the professional knowledge of the dominated which confirmed their superiority. The aristocratic hero of Baroness Orczy's *The Scarlet Pimpernel*, 1905, displays his super-iority to his French revolutionary adversaries of both sexes by his capacity to impersonate them. Sherlock Holmes has similar abilities. Kim's attachment to the lama is presented as a serious attraction to Oriental wisdom, but in 1903 Conan Doyle redeployed the theme when he had Holmes tell Watson in 'The Empty House' that he had spent the two years since his apparent death at the Reichenbach Falls hiding out in a Tibetan lamasery.

The narrative voice of *Kim* mimics the inclusiveness of the hero who is heir to all Eurasia. Situated somewhere between West and East, with an archaic floridity that purports to mimic the Oriental and is starkly contrasted by the terseness of the British characters, it suggests Kim's ability 'to enter another's soul'. It celebrates the professional knowledge of the Westerner, who acquires his superiority over the inferior other by his ability to impersonate him. The novel offers a genial justification of the idea of a permanent Raj, by demonstrating that the rich cultural diversity of the subcontinent is best preserved by those British who are receptive to Indian cultures. Kim's experiences as a native supremely fit him for the Great Game and the defence of British hegemony.

For Kim the possibility of genuine openness seems to remain until his meeting with the Woman of Shamlegh in the penultimate chapter. Up to this point the only female character has been the grandmotherly Sahiba. Western society appears as entirely masculine; there are no European women characters. Indian society, with its emphasis on sexual intrigues, is feminised; manly Indians join the masculine society of the Great Game. Kim's sexually charged meeting with the Woman, head-woman in her hill village but with past experience of a Western lover, confirms the end of his childhood and the limits of the romance genre. The introduction of sexuality into the work, with its reminder of the impossibility of miscegenation, destroys the fiction of openness which *Kim* has hitherto indulged. There is a recognition that now Kim is sexually mature he must join the Western masculine Great Game.

Kipling's later Edwardian work, like Conrad's, recognised two distinct audiences: that for innovative fiction and that for romance. Like Conrad he experimented with multiple narrators; the most extreme example was the short story 'Mrs Bathurst', 1904, where narrators from the far-flung battlelines of empire construct a story as resistant to easy understanding as *Lord Jim*. On the other hand *Puck of Pook's Hill*, 1906, was intended to introduce children younger than those who might read *Kim* to the history of imperial Britain.

At the beginning of *Heart of Darkness* Marlow imagines the time when Britain was one of the dark places of the earth to Roman imperialists. Kipling realised this reversal in the Roman stories of *Puck*, but within the form of juvenile romance. The listeners within the story are two modern children, the teller a young Roman recruit who has himself little concept of the workings of empire beyond his own duties defending Hadrian's Wall. In the wider empire, it is suggested, are vast intrigues; only the limits of the narrator's vision, and that of the listeners, permit the material to be presented in tales of heroic adventurism.

In presenting Britain as an offshore outpost of empire threatened by darkness, Kipling is in tune with the pervasive fears expressed in the 'invasion literature' of the period. This subgenre, imagining an England open to invasion, went back to the 1870s, but contemporary debates about military preparedness, including the Dreadnought crisis of 1906, assured its revived popularity.[30] These fictions shifted the emphasis from imperial adventure overseas to the threatened heart of empire. The major example of invasion scare fiction, Erskine Childers' *The Riddle of the Sands*, 1903, is, like *Kim* and *The Secret Agent*, an early spy thriller, and it was into this most popular genre of the twentieth century that the matter of empire passed. *Kim* provided the positive model on which later writers such as John Buchan and Ian Fleming depended; *The Secret Agent*, the negative model, was followed by the spy fictions of Graham Greene.

CRITICS OF EMPIRE: SHAW, WELLS, FORSTER

Finding an audience appropriately receptive to criticisms of imperialism in this period could be difficult as the curious stage history of

Shaw's play, *John Bull's Other Island*, first performed in 1904, proved. Set in England's ancient colony, Ireland, it was originally written at Yeats's request for performance at Dublin's Abbey Theatre, and its purpose was to warn the Irish of the strength of English imperialism, and of the dangers of responding to that threat by a retreat into Celtic romanticism. The main English character, Broadbent, is a Liberal businessman committed to Home Rule for Ireland who regrets the submerging of his own 'dear old island' in 'this confounded new Empire'.[31] He is also a practical exponent of green imperialism, assuming the economic dominance of a district of Ireland with the willing help of the locals, his exceptional business acumen enhanced by his sentimental appreciation of Irish culture.

Shaw's criticism of Irish acquiescence in English imperialism is effected through a manipulation of the conventions of Irish senti-mental drama.[32] The Irish characters are all from stock, playing sentimental roles to beguile the dominant race, examples of how oppressed people accept and internalise the roles allotted them by their rulers. Broadbent, in contrast, is an extreme example of self-confidence and imperviousness to criticism. Shaw's presentation of the Irish as a colonised people indulging in fantasies of forging an identity antithetical to that of capitalist, imperialist England was, however, rejected by Yeats who was committed to just such a notion of Irish identity. Later it was Shaw's first flop with audiences in the States, who are traditionally sympathetic to Irish themes.

In England, moreover, it proved impossible to enforce an imperialist critique on the West End theatre audience who received Broadbent's imperviousness warmly. The play was Shaw's first big success in England. Arthur Balfour, the Prime Minister, saw it five times, inviting other political leaders to the theatre and urging its importance on them. There was also a royal command perform-ance.[33] To the audience in the stalls, as Shaw's Preface suggested, the play seemed to be a celebration of English imperial guile and efficiency, and of an ability to rule other races through understand-ing their cultures.

Another socialist critique of imperialism appears in Wells's *Tono-Bungay*, 1909, a 'condition-of-England' novel (see Chapter 3), with one episode of imperial adventurism. The hero, George Ponderevo, seeks to recover the failing fortunes of his uncle's business by cornering the world's supply of a radioactive substance called quap. For this episode, in which George attempts to realise a dream of world economic domination, Wells adopted a romance narrative form, loosely modelled on *Heart of Darkness*. George's ship sets out for the African coast with a crew apparently recruited from the *Narcissus* and a pessimistic East European captain, possibly a reference to Conrad. He moves into a world where normal motive disappears. When George murders an African, the act takes place outside any context of reference he can recognise. The ship heads for England with its radioactive cargo, but the Ponderevos' dream of world domination fades when the ship disintegrates in mid-ocean. English imperialist ideas of conquest and efficiency are revealed as mere fantasy.

The major liberal anti-imperialist fiction of the period is E. M. Forster's *A Passage to India*, not published till 1924, but first drafted in 1912. Its inattention to Indian nationalist movements, and its acceptance of the opposition of Western efficiency and Eastern inefficiency, are characteristic of the imperial fiction of this period. As in *Kim* a dream of male inter-racial friendship crossing imperial barriers is disrupted by the presence of women, and the memsahib is seen as the prime explanation for imperialism's enforcement of distance between the races.

Edwardian fiction explored the beginnings of a crisis of imperial identity. The invulnerable and privileged English hero was to survive in popular fiction, but he survived longest in the defensive form of the spy thriller. The major fictions of the period suggested the dangers of implicit reliance on imperial privilege, and foresaw that the English would soon urgently need to discover a new national identity.

Chapter 3

'The condition of England'

The Edwardian period saw a number of attempts to provide the kind of wide-ranging social commentary found in writings of the early and middle Victorian period. One influential work of social analysis, *The Condition of England*, 1909, by the Liberal politician Charles Masterman, used Carlyle's famous phrase as its title. Masterman's survey found a country poised on the brink of irreversible change, where the unknown urban masses threatened to bring about a permanent but unpredictable mutation in the national identity. His picture of 'our civilisation as a little patch of redeemed land in the wilderness', menaced as by 'the rush of a bank-holiday crowd upon some tranquil garden', is central to the worries of the period. So is his identification of the 'real' England with rural England, and his fear that 'the reconstruction of a rural civilisation' was rapidly becoming an impossibility.[1]

The writers who analysed the 'condition of England' were mostly hostile to the idea of imperial England, and sought to define an alternative and pre-existing national identity, to locate the 'real' England far away from the frontiers of empire, and usually in rural areas. In reformulating the condition-of-England question as the proper matter for the writer, they often looked back to the methods of the Victorian panoramic novel, and their writings sought to define a real, if slumbering, community which only needed to be given information to make it interest itself in England's acute problems. 'Only connect. . .', the epigraph of E. M. Forster's *Howards End*, could serve as the general epigraph for these writings, as it could for the Condition of England novels of the 1840s and 1850s.

LIBERAL COMMENTARIES: *HOWARDS END* AND *STRIFE*

Howards End, 1910, is deeply hostile to the dominant definition of national identity as imperialist and masculine. It shows a society polarised by assumptions that most activities are gender-specific. The heroine early outlines this problem:

> 'I suppose that ours is a female house,' said Margaret 'and one must just accept it. No, Aunt Juley, I don't mean that this house is full of women. I am trying to say something much more clever. I mean that it was irrevocably feminine even in father's time . . . it must be feminine, and all we can do is to see that it isn't effeminate. Just as another house that I can mention, but won't, sounded irrevocably masculine, and all its inmates can do is to see that it isn't brutal.'[2]

The purpose of the novel was to imagine the reincorporation in the important life of the country of those activities defined as feminine. The ruling class is represented by the Wilcox family whose men are types of the masculine imperialist character dominant in English society. Their defensiveness is characterised by frequent images of barricades and fortifications. Culture and personal relations, excluded from this masculine world, have become feminised; they are represented in the novel by the Schlegel sisters and their effeminate brother.

By bringing the Wilcoxes and Schlegels into alliance and emphasising the need for the masculine and feminine sides of English society to reconnect, Forster was attempting to reconstruct the organic society described in English novels of the eighteenth and nineteenth centuries. He rejected the new imperial England as a facade which had imposed itself upon the traditional rural England represented by the small country house. The scene where Margaret goes to dine with Mr Wilcox at Simpson's in the Strand shows the two mythologies opposed:

her eyes surveyed the restaurant, and admired its well-calculated tributes to the solidity of our past. Though no more Old English than the works of Kipling, it had selected its reminiscences so adroitly that her criticism was lulled, and the guests whom it was nourishing for imperial purposes bore the outer resemblance of Parson Adams or Tom Jones. Scraps of their talk jarred oddly on the ear. 'Right you are! I'll cable out to Uganda this evening,' came from the table behind. (Ch. 17)

V. S. Naipaul discusses this scene in his An Area of Darkness:

He [Forster] has pointed out the contradiction in the myth of a people overtaken by industry and imperial power . . . at the height of their power the British gave the impression of a people at play, a people playing at being English, playing at being English of a certain class . . . always between the protected adjustable myth – Parson Adams in Simpson's, the harassed empire-builder in Uganda or India – and the reality, there is some distance.[3]

By using Old English mythology the people engaged in running the British Empire were to remain disengaged from the realities of the imperial situation. The continual slippage from 'British', with its implications of empire, to 'English', with its more traditional and rural associations, was a useful part of the armament of invulnerability.

Forster was conscious of this slippage, as the Simpson's passage shows, but he was anxious to assert the real continuing existence of a traditional rural England to which the imperialists who use its imagery are overmasculinised mutants. His problem was to distinguish Old English from old English; as Naipaul points out, the imperialists had captured the imagery of Englishness, and its perpetuation could be seen as no more than a particular manner of asserting English/British distinctiveness. Many themes were common to imperialists and to Howards End, for instance the regret for a lost or declining yeomanry.

Forster's project was to reconstruct an organic community, not one bound by the ideological cement of imperialism. His concept of Englishness readmitted the female and the European. The Schlegels, who are half-German, though critical of Germany's own imperialism, represent a wider European culture. Imperialism excluded women, while offering hopes of participation to men below the ruling class.

Forster's redefinition of community had problems accommodating the lower middle, and working classes in their existing form.

The famous opening of Chapter 6 raises the question of whether the insurance clerk, Leonard Bast, can be incorporated in the community addressed. 'We are not concerned with the very poor. They are unthinkable and only to be approached by the statistician or the poet. The story deals with gentlefolk, or with those who are obliged to pretend that they are gentlefolk.' Leonard 'was not in the abyss but he could see it'; he is seen by Forster as being on the very edge of knowable society, that is, on the very edge of any definition of the 'we' who are 'not concerned'.

N. N. Feltes, in his *Modes of Production of Victorian Novels*, suggests that Forster's problem with the pronoun 'we' is exemplary of authorial uncertainties, common at the period, about the nature of the reading public.[4] The major shift in publishing conditions, the growth of the audience for fiction, and its increasing specialisation, presented difficulties to the novelist seeking to invoke the kind of community of shared assumptions which had been addressed in the authorial commentaries of the great Victorian novelists. Forster's uncertainties about the precise inclusiveness of that community made his definition of that 'we' very shifting. It is not clear who is excluded and who addressed.

If Leonard's inclusion is marginal and uncertain, his wife, Jacky, is an obvious candidate for exclusion. As an ex-prostitute she belongs to the abyss and is, therefore, 'unthinkable'. Jacky is not only 'unthinkable' but 'bestially stupid' (Ch. 26), and thus incapable of imagining her own state. In contrast the junior Wilcox wife, Dolly, is at least permitted self-knowledge. 'She was a rubbishy little creature and she knew it' (Ch. 11). It is apparently Dolly's class status which allows her that awareness of moral distinctions implied in putative membership of the community of 'we'.

Clearly Jacky can never be part of the English community which Forster was seeking to reconstruct; Leonard's exclusion is more problematic. When he walks in the countryside his responses are constrained by a literary construction of Old England as synthetic as that of the imperialists. He is, however, 'grandson to the shepherd or ploughboy whom civilisation had sucked into the town' (Ch. 14).

He represents the 'lost' peasantry, and is therefore appropriately the father of the Schlegel child who will inherit Howards End, replacing the imperialist Wilcox with a traditional, rural model derived from the organic community Forster was seeking to invoke. In person, however, Leonard and the lower middle class he represents can have no place in this reconstructed community; they are a failed experiment which must be eliminated as Leonard himself is at the end of the story.

Howards End represents the point of view of those writers who rejected the new imperialist England and sought to look back beyond the Empire to an organic England. Forster's recognition of the need to assert that England's distinction from the Old England of the imperialists is shown in the fantasy elements of the writing, the conscious mythologising associated with the English countryside, and with the mother–goddess figure of Ruth Wilcox. The claim that 'England still waits for the supreme moment of her literature' (Ch. 33) is an attempt to look forward as well as back, and create a synthesis of the old realism and the new mythologising. Forster did not solve the problem of integrating the fantasy with the traditional realist parts of the novel, and the pastoralism does not distinguish itself recognisably from that of the books Leonard is criticised for reading.

Howards End marked the crisis both for liberal humanism and for traditional realism.[5] After the war Forster finished *A Passage to India*, but wrote no more novels. If the project of *Howards End* sometimes seems to dwindle to little more than an insistence that the business community should get together with the cultured section of the middle class, this may be ascribed to Forster's inability to break from the methods of the Victorian social panoramic novel, despite his lack of confidence in their continuing appropriateness. His admission of his extensive areas of ignorance, and the shifting nature of the boundaries he describes between 'us' and 'them', undermine his attempts to claim an authority like that of the Victorian social commentators. His attempt to invoke a community distinct from the gendered exclusivenesss of imperialism founders on his uncertainties about the nature of his audience.

One of the most influential histories of the Edwardian period, George Dangerfield's *The Strange Death of Liberal England*, describes the terminal crisis of liberalism as the central event of the period. That crisis, as liberalism sought to find a viable position in an increasingly polarised society, is demonstrated in *Howards End*, and in a play by another liberal writer of the period, John Galsworthy's *Strife*. This play was first performed in 1909 and was considered sufficiently relevant to contemporary perceptions of industrial conflict for BBC Television to give it two productions in the last fifteen years.

Strife is, like *Howards End*, an attempt to 'connect', in this case a West End theatre audience with the unfamiliar subject of an industrial dispute. The setting, a tin plate works on the Welsh border, describes the division between management and work force in terms also of a racial division between English and Welsh. The English chairman is characterised as reserved, terse, communicating his instructions in undertones; the Welsh leader of the dispute is excitable and eloquent, and the emotionalism of the Welsh characters marks them as subjected both in race and in class.

Galsworthy's ostensible purpose is to endorse the position of the moderates in his play and to urge the need for understanding and compromise on his middle-class audience. His plays, which also included his plea for prison reform, *Justice*, 1910, were valued by the Fabians Beatrice and Sidney Webb for their attempts to sway policy by communicating necessary facts to an audience of the influential.[6] *Strife* appears to be offering its well-connected West End audience something to do, ways of understanding, and working for, a less divided community.

In effect however, the play privileges the extremist characters over the moderates. Before the moderates force a compromise solution, both the chairman and the strike leader make rhetorically similar speeches, foreseeing an apocalyptic future if their cause is lost. The Welshman's Act II plea to his workmates that they should not 'help to blacken the sky' is followed by the chairman's warning in Act III of 'the future of this country, threatened with the black waters of confusion'.[7] At the end, as the moderates tidy up, the two antagonists, both defeated, silently salute each other, a sentimental gesture on Galsworthy's part which completes the undoing of his apparent polemic purpose.

SOCIALIST COMMENTARIES: TRESSELL AND LONDON

The excluded voice from the abyss is heard most strongly in the classic working-class novel of the period, Robert Tressell's *The Ragged Trousered Philanthropists*, 1914. Tressell, a house-painter whose real name was Robert Noonan, wrote a 'condition-of-England' novel for a very different community from the one *Howards End* attempts to address. Tressell pointedly excludes the middle class as audience. The middle-class figures who appear in the novel as employers and local politicians are taken from stock, Dickensian stereotypes on whom Dickens may safely be presumed to have said the last word.

Tressell's insistence that novels can have nothing further illuminating to say about these people is compounded by his treatment of dialogue. He observes a convention whereby the employer class speak an English more illiterate and uneducated than that of the house-painters they employ and exploit, while Owen, the socialist, working-class hero and his family speak the standard English conventionally associated with virtue in Victorian novels. In Tressell's novel the crisis of liberalism central to *Howards End* is represented only by the marginal figure of the local councillor, Dr Weakling, a man with no real constituency, who loses his seat before the end of the book.

The Ragged Trousered Philanthropists is a novel about the search for a working-class audience, and the methods by which that audience might be created. Like *Howards End* it is seeking to define and construct a community. Its publication history did not follow the conventional route. Three years after Noonan/Tressell died in a workhouse in 1911, his manuscript was revised and drastically abridged for publication by the writer Jessie Pope, otherwise best known to literary history as the person whose sentimental war poetry provoked Wilfred Owen's 'Dulce et Decorum Est'. After its appearance in 1914 Tressell's novel spent a long period as an underground classic distributed through working-class networks. Only in 1955 was the complete version published.[8]

In recounting the attempts of Frank Owen to convert his fellow workers to socialism, The Ragged Trousered Philanthropists takes as its subject the attempt to construct an audience. The reader is insistently reminded of the general context of information to which the book seeks to act as antidote. This information is provided by the Church, the press, and the music-hall, the imperialist bias of which is mimicked in the 'Pandorama' at the children's party in Chapter 29.

We are given numerous examples of the kinds of text available to Owen's working-class audience, from the newspapers from which Owen's colleagues collect clippings to refute him, to the halfpenny romances which lead nursemaids literally astray in Chapter 43. The pervasive presence of the popular songs of the period, including hymns and election songs, is registered in the many quotations from them. The different forms of writing with which the characters would be most familiar are reproduced in full: minutes, sandwich-board advertisements, timesheets, posters for meetings. Owen's talks, like the Socialist literature which he distributes, are struggling for an audience in competition with these other forms of writing and speech.

Owen's speeches are given in full in the novel, but are placed very firmly in the context of the response of their immediate audience. In this respect the novel resembles another polemic novel of the period, Elizabeth Robins's suffragette novel The Convert, 1907 (see Chapter 5). Both writers are speaking for marginalised constituencies, and their acute awareness of the problems of holding audiences, the techniques needed, and the kinds of reception possible, are part of the subject of their work. Owen's orations are not detachable from their context; the audience response, the hostility, the counter citation of newspaper clippings, the English working-class worries about the fate of the royal family in a socialist future, are an integral part of the process described.

Jessie Pope's abridgement of The Ragged Trousered Philanthropists ended with the prospect of Owen's suicide, directing the book towards a pathos presumably intended for middle-class readers. The full version ends more positively with Owen's family surviving the winter on a loan from his workmate Barrington, now revealed as a middle-class socialist in disguise. For Tressell's intended audience it was crucial that his hero, and especially his hero's child, survive. The child is the heir for England on whom, as in *Howards End*, the future depends.

The need for a positive ending, however, involved Tressell in difficulties. The house-painting trade was not unionised, so Tressell had no means of suggesting a strong supportive community among the workers.[9] The particular condition of Owen's own political awareness and articulacy is his status as one of the few remaining craftsmen, trained in a dying tradition. After excluding middle-class intervention throughout the book Tressell had to let Barrington bail Owen out, and also affirm his solidarity by giving the last and longest speech in the book, the 'Great Oration'. The resolution Tressell found was outside the working-class community he was addressing.

Jack London's autobiographical *The People of the Abyss*, 1903, is a Socialist account of an attempt to 'connect' with the unknown working class of London by going 'down and out', as George Orwell was to do thirty years later. London, an American, came to England as a reporter to cover the Boer War, but stayed at the heart of empire, and attempted to understand the London working-class community by immersing himself in it. His book is a record of failure, of the impossibility of connecting. What London claimed to find was a new race who had lost the characteristics of the English, and whose area of habitation he might thus appropriately call a ghetto.

London's account realised the fears of the critics of imperialism that the people at the heart of empire were going native. The documentary form he adopted presented itself as a scientific investigation into the racial mutants being produced by the unnatural life of the city. He reported that 'a new race has sprung up, a street people. . . . The traditional silent and reserved Englishman has passed away. The pavement folk are noisy, voluble, high-strung, excitable'.[10] In departing from the racial characteristics of the imperial Englishman the London working class had become foreigners, and their foreignness derived specifically from their urban nature. In the chapter called 'The Sea Wife', London interviewed an old countrywoman whose many sons were variously dispersed around the empire, an unchanged race of real Englishmen whose places could not be filled. The heart of empire itself was running out of men.

IMAGES OF RURAL ENGLAND: UTOPIAS, LAWRENCE

Jack London's discovery that England was running out of real people, specifically men to whom excitability was alien, is reiterated throughout the literature of the period. Forster's policy in *Howards End* was to write off the members of the existing urban population represented by Leonard Bast, and to redefine them as lost plough-boys, allowed a possible future by the hope that Leonard's son will recreate that lost world.

Images of an idealised rural past proliferate in this age of imperialism and of the Aliens Act. The poetic sleeper of the decade was A. E. Housman's *A Shropshire Lad*, 1896; George Orwell, analysing the appeal to his generation of this series of pastoral lyrics, found it in the fact that 'the *rentier*-professional class was ceasing once and for all to have any relationship with the soil'.[11] The same readership assured the success of the pastoral Georgian poets at the end of the decade. In this context it was not so much the specific novels or poems of Thomas Hardy that made him significant, but his availability as a rural icon, as 'our most genuine, most autochthonous of living poets',[12] (see Chapter 6). Even Hardy's longevity contributed significantly to his status as surviving aboriginal of Old England.

The insistence that the *real* England was rural England colonised various forms of literature. The travel book metamorphosed into the commercially popular English heritage book, recounting journeys around a rapidly disappearing rural England. Edward Thomas made a living from this newly popular genre with such books as *The Heart of England*, 1906, *The South Country*, 1909, and *The Icknield Way*, 1911, and later reworked the material in the poetry he wrote after the outbreak of World War I. The long tradition of country-house literature dwindled down to the first of the country-house whodunits, E. C. Bentley's *Trent's Last Case*, 1913, ossifying in a genre which was to flourish between the wars.

The children's classics of the period also addressed themselves to Old England. In Kenneth Grahame's *The Wind in the Willows*, 1908, a group of leisured, landowning bachelors, exposed to working-class insurrection through the fashionable motoring illegalities of a member of their group, successfully fight back to expel the intruders from the ancient seats they have occupied and manage to retain their former privileges. Secure within his fantasy genre, Grahame revealed even the rural working class, the stoats and weasels, to be potential insurrectionaries, and restored a countryside thoroughly cowed by the gentlemen. Frances Hodgson Burnett, in *The Secret Garden*, 1911, was truer to the Victorian fictional tradition in suggesting the interdependence of the classes. Her story advocated a return to a properly responsible squirearchy, with the young heir to the manor restored to health and *noblesse oblige* by instruction in rural lore from a juvenile Pan among his tenantry.

In Edwardian additions to the new genre of science fiction the lost peasantry were frequently predicted as the desirable people of the future. In Forster's own attempt at the genre, the short story 'The Machine Stops', 1909, the Homeless of Wessex lurk many ages outside the subterranean machine city, waiting to rebuild a kingdom once more in direct contact with the earth.[13] Forster's machine city was intended as a liberal humanist response to the urban, socialist, technological Utopias of Wells, but the dream of a future of revitalised peasants was common to the political left and right as well.

Wells's novel, *The War in the Air*, 1908, concludes its account of a world destroyed in a war of aerial bombardment with a description of the survivors, 'squatters among the clay and oak thickets of the Weald'.[14] Although Wells, as socialist and modern, stresses the precariousness of this peasant existence, his squatters nevertheless represent a way of life more secure and happy than that of the world they replace. On the right Kipling, in his 1912 story 'As Easy as

ABC', another attack on Wellsian Utopias, imagined a planet decimated by democratic wars, where the people live in thousand-acre farms or in small market towns like 'innocent, contented little Chicago', but where the memory of urban crowding and democratic politics can still produce blind panic.[15]

While the dominance of the rural possibility in popular genres was significant for later developments, its continuance in the mainstream tradition of the novel was signalled in 1911 with the publication of Lawrence's first novel, The White Peacock. The novel is set in an idyllic rural valley, and a Panlike gamekeeper presides over the first half of the story, but the idyll is corrupted by the characters' awareness of lost wisdom, of the 'old wild lost religion'.[16] The death of the gamekeeper, who best understands this, and denounces modern civilisation as 'the painted fungus of rottenness' (Part II, Ch. 2), confirms the loss. The flirtations with socialism of the principal character, George, are futile, but as a man he cannot accept the archaic rural life still available to his sister.

The allures and metamorphoses of the pastoral are examined in the chapter 'Pastorals and peonies'. The narrator has earlier heard the gamekeeper's story of his marriage, a tortured misalliance with an aristocrat, a 'white peacock'. Later at a polite picnic he tells a female audience the story of a hedge-cutter who accidentally shot the aristocrat lady he loved when she crept up on him in the garden pretending to be a fairy. This prettily poetic version of the miseries of the gamekeeper's class misalliance is very successful with his hearers. In softening the vigour of the gamekeeper's man-to-man story to the daintiness of the ladies' edition, Lawrence suggested that the specialisation of the fiction audience was part of the decay in civilisation he was recording.

Lawrence in his earlier work encountered the same problem as Forster and other writers who sought to invoke an old England distinct from the Old England of the imperialists. In the story 'England, my England', 1915, he attempted a definition of the sense of national identity which his hero feels as he goes to war, an identity which is quite distinct from that of the imperialists:

He had not the faintest desire to overcome any foreigners or to help in their death. He had no conception of Imperial England, and Rule Britannia was just a joke to him. He was a pure-blooded Englishman, perfect in his race, and when he was truly himself he could no more have been aggressive on the score of his Englishness than a rose can be aggressive on the score of its rosiness.[17]

The distinction was one which many writers of the period struggled to maintain, insisting on an old England from which the imperialists' England was an aberration. The distinction was a fine one; the imperialists were themselves celebrating aboriginal England. Rider Haggard's long documentary survey, *Rural England*, 1902, lamented the disappearance of the English yeoman. In this decade Kipling turned from India to Sussex, and in such stories as 'Below the Mill-Dam', 1902, 'An Habitation Enforced', 1905, and the tales of *Puck of Pook's Hill*, 1906, found the real England in the continuity of English rural life.

THE COUNTRY-HOUSE TRADITION: *TONO-BUNGAY*

The England of Edwardian writings is a peculiar geographical entity. There are exceptions, such as *The White Peacock*, but it is usually defined as the Home Counties. The myth is of England, not Britain, of a non-political, cultural entity in which Scotland and Wales, the earliest subjects of imperial expansion, figure uneasily, and in which the more outlying parts of England itself have only a tenuous existence. In *Howards End* Margaret and Wilcox reject the idea of living in Shropshire (rural, gentrified, but too far from the core), and return to Hertfordshire. Englishness in this period tends to be defined by nearness to London and the Home Counties, to the centre of gentry power and the Crown. It does not, however, reside in London itself, that rapidly evolving heart of empire.

Wells's most important novel, *Tono-Bungay*, 1909, analysed the gentry life of the Home Counties as the emblematic concentration of the real England. Bladesover, the great country house in which his hero grows up in the servant quarters as the housekeeper's son, is offered as the central myth for understanding England, the myth which precludes the dynamic restructuring Britain needs to survive in the modern world. Even those parts of England which do not conform to the Bladesover model confirm its dominance, as the narrator explains in a passage which evokes Jane Austen's comparison of Mansfield Park and Portsmouth:

> I have never revisited Chatham; the impression it has left on my mind is one of squalid compression, unlit by any gleam of a maturer charity. All its effects arranged themselves as antithetical to the Bladesover effects. They confirmed and intensified all that Bladesover suggested. Bladesover declared itself to be the land, to be essentially England; I have already told how its airy spaciousness, its wide dignity, seemed to thrust village, church and vicarage into corners, into a secondary and conditional significance. Here one gathered the corollary of that. Since the whole wide country of Kent was made up of contiguous Bladesovers and for the gentlefolk, the surplus of population, all who were not good tenants nor good labourers, Church of England, submissive and respectful, were necessarily thrust together, jostled out of sight, to fester as they might in this place that had the colours and even the smells of a well-packed dustbin. They should be grateful even for that; that, one felt, was the theory of it all.[18]

Wells wrote *Tono-Bungay* in the country-house tradition of literature in order to expose the distorting and imprisoning effect the Bladesover dominance has on English life. Bladesover proliferates through the English society of this social, panoramic novel. In London the hero finds only recognisable variants of the Bladesover system; 'this idea of escaping parts from the seventeenth-century system of Bladesover, of proliferating and overgrowing elements from the Estates . . . to this day seems to me the best explanation, not simply of London, but of all England' (Part II, Ch. 1).

The narrator of *Tono-Bungay* anticipates the imminent demise of the Bladesover myth, its 'fine foliage of pretences' exposed to the frosts of the modern world. The continuing proliferation and dominance of images of Howards End and Bladesover to represent Englishness have proved this anticipation premature. When Bladesover's original, Uppark, where Wells's mother had been housekeeper, burned down in September 1989, the extensive newspaper commentaries on its past associations scarcely mentioned the creator of Bladesover. And this omission bears out Wells's contention that the servants' hall has no place in the myth of Englishness.

The continuing relevance of Wells's Bladesover thesis has also been variously endorsed by two recent controversial political analyses of English culture. Martin Wiener's *English Culture and the Decline of the Industrial Spirit*, an influential American critique of a Britain stifled by a myth of rural gentry England, presents as its epigraph Wells's insistence that 'Bladesover is . . . the clue to all that is distinctively British and perplexing to the foreign inquirer in England' (Part I, Ch. 1).[19] Tom Nairn's analysis of the myth of the monarchy and its functions, *The Enchanted Glass*, expands on the idea of England as defined by the Crown and Home Counties gentry. This 'romantic concentrate', Nairn suggests, received its definitive formulation at the turn of the century. 'The epoch depicted in *Tono-Bungay* is that where the totemisation of Queen Victoria coincided exactly with London's definitive take-over of provincial Britain and the fabrication of a High Imperialist variant of "Greatness." '[20]

In *Tono-Bungay* Bladesover does not represent the continuing strength of the real England, but rather a morbid proliferation which must be destroyed. The traditions of the social panoramic novel which represented Bladesover culture are also displayed by Wells as moving to disintegration.[21] *Howards End*, solving the 'condition-of-England' question by affirming the myth of the country house, is a well-made novel, its successes determined by its continuity with an existing tradition. *Tono-Bungay*, rejecting the myths of an ordered society which sustain the traditional novel, proliferates in episodic form. The hero, jolted out of his place in the class structure, confesses he can find no existing means to present himself as a unified identity. With the imminent and desirable loss of the structuring myth goes the loss of the possibility for coherent relations and motivations. Wells's major novel suggested that the existing myths and literary forms which described England were no longer viable in the twentieth century.

Chapter 4

The importance of parricide

Generational revolt is a major theme in the literature of the Edwardian period. The insistence that a new age was establishing itself found expression in novels and plays which described a young protagonist's attempt to rebel against the heavy inheritance of Victorianism, and the patriarchs or matriarchs who represented it. With this went a determination to escape the conventions of the novel of social realism which had portrayed Victorian society, and to explore new forms which were more open and more responsive to the inner life of the individual. These reactions were part of late Victorianism, but the new century gave added impetus to their expression. The particular manifestations of female rebellion in literature against the Victorian inheritance will be examined in the next chapter; this chapter will describe the general popularity of the rebel child as hero.

In 1913 D. H. Lawrence said 'We have to hate our immediate predecessors, to get free from their authority.' [1] The Edwardians followed this dictum with particular vigour. Filial revolt was an important part of the assertion of manliness in literature. To the next generation, to whom World War I had given overwhelming motives for rejecting the authority of their fathers, the established literary figures of the Edwardian period appeared as especially oppressive patriarchs. But these writers saw themselves as rebels engaged in a life-or-death struggle to repudiate the Victorian inheritance. Although Freud's writings did not become well known in Britain till after the First World War, when they provided the moderns with explanations of and methods of describing their own revolt, the Edwardian writers pursued their collective Oedipal rebellion against the Victorians in parallel with Freud.

BENNETT: CLAYHANGER

Arnold Bennett became a prime example of the tyranny of patriarchal realism to the postwar generation, as 'Mr Nixon', the venal and worldly father-figure of Ezra Pound's *Hugh Selwyn Mauberley*, or as the novelist most frequently cited by Virginia Woolf to represent the heavy fathers of the realist novel. Bennett, however, was anxious to repudiate his Victorian literary inheritance, adopting ancestors from outside England: Turgenev, Flaubert, Maupassant, Zola. He was also anxious to distinguish himself from his middle-class readership. In a 1909 article, 'Middle-class', he described 'the great, stolid, comfortable class which forms the backbone of the novel-reading public', and his own position as someone who had entered the class from below, but had then voluntarily exiled himself from it. 'I know it intimately, nearly all the intimacy being on my side. For I have watched it during long, agreeable, sardonic months and years in foreign hotels.' [2] He was also an exile from his provincial roots, like Joyce adopting the view that exile was the only possible condition for the artist.

Bennett's major Edwardian novels, *Anna of the Five Towns*, 1902, *The Old Wives' Tale*, 1908, *Clayhanger*, 1910, and its sequel *Hilda Lessways*, 1911, describe rebellions against parents. The heavy furniture which crowds his extensively detailed rooms, like that in the elaborate stage directions of the plays of the period, indicates the sheer weight of the material inheritance with which his young protagonists had to contend. Early in *Clayhanger*, there is a description of the spatial disposition of the patriarchal family:

> The position of Mr Clayhanger's easy-chair – a detail apparently trifling – was in reality a strongly influencing factor in the family life, for it meant that the father's presence obsessed the room. . . . When the children reflected upon the history of their childhood they saw one

important aspect of it as a long series of detached hours spent in the sitting-room, in a state of desire to do something that could not be done without disturbing father, and in a state of indecision whether or not to disturb him. If by chance, as sometimes occurred, he chose to sit on the sofa, which was unobtrusive in the corner away from the window, between the fireplace and the door, the room was instantly changed into something larger, freer, and less inconvenient.[3]

Bennett's anxiety to register the intense pressure of circumstance upon his characters was interpreted by Woolf as gross materialism. In her 1924 article, 'Mr Bennett and Mrs Brown', Bennett was her major example of the Edwardian novelists' who laid 'enormous stress upon the fabric of things',[4] who provided excessive amounts of material detail about the houses in which the characters lived, and who failed to find means of realising the inner lives of the characters. Woolf linked the cumbersome and restricting realism of the Edwardian novels to the patriarchal attitudes of the writers who produced them, and Bennett for her represented the patriarchal writer who ignored his characters' spirit in his attempt to describe their circumstances. The Edwardian novel to Woolf was the last monument to realism, an elaborately detailed house in which no real humanity existed. The postwar novel, attentive to the inner spirit, was a more open arrangement, 'larger, freer, and less inconvenient'.

Bennett's earlier novels, *Anna of the Five Towns* and *The Old Wives' Tale*, are realist novels which describe the failure of daughters to break effectively from the social world of their fathers. *Clayhanger*, which describes a son's more successful revolt against a patriarch, is in transition from realism. Bennett's move away from the preoccupations of realism is clearly related to the gender of his protagonist. *Clayhanger* is the story of how Edwin Clayhanger, son of a successful self-made printer, rejects the Victorian ideal represented by his dynamic father in favour of a life of aesthetic sensation, and fulfilment through leisure and love.[5]

We are told in the second chapter that 'in that head of his a flame burnt that was like an altar-fire, a miraculous and beautiful phenomenon', and throughout the novel Edwin learns to live as Pater recommended in the 'Conclusion' to *The Renaissance*, 1873, using every moment to discriminate the exquisite in the circumstances around him. We are not invited to worry much about his failure to pursue the artistic career of which he briefly dreams, still less about his half-hearted management of the business his father founded. Edwin's justification lies in the intensity of his aesthetic response, to the new hot-water system, which 'affected and inspired Edwin like a poem' (Part II, Ch. 4), to the journals he 'began to read, as it were, voluptuously' (Part III, Ch. 1), and to the 'exquisite burden' (Part IV, Ch. 13) of Hilda, the woman he loves.

In launching his hero on this Paterian career Bennett endorses Pater's description of the impressionistic nature of experience. 'Experience, already reduced to a group of impressions, is ringed round for each one of us by that thick wall of personality through which no real voice has ever pierced on its way to us'.[6] Despite the elaborate detail of its environment, this novel rejects the social panoramic realism of the Victorian novel. The political and social life of the Potteries is excluded except in so far as it provides background material for Edwin's reveries, as with the unrest in the streets during a potters' strike; 'all that grim, perilous background only gave to his emotions a further intensity, troubling them to still stranger ecstasy' (Part II, Ch. 21). A detailed description of the printing-works is part of a courtship ritual with Hilda, just as in *Anna of the Five Towns*, a pottery works serves the same purpose.

The rejection of Victorian social realism is made clear with the treatment of Chapters 4 and 5 in Part I which describe the early life of Edwin's father, Darius. The narrative of Darius's childhood as a pottery worker, and in the workhouse, provides the kind of social material and criticism found in the great Victorian novels of social realism. But it is isolated from the rest of the book, as an episode deep in Darius's memory, and unknown to the contemporary world of the novel. It is specifically unknown to Edwin who has been kept entirely ignorant of his father's past.

For these chapters Bennett drew very heavily on the memoir *When I Was a Child*, 1903, by the ex-pottery worker, Charles Shaw, allowing the older generation to speak for themselves, and thus further distinguishing these pages from those around them. The isolation of this episode, which is powerful and moving in the manner of Victorian realism, suggests that such narratives can only be incorporated in contemporary experience as picturesque and nostalgic anecdotes. There is no belief in the ability of the novel to oversee the wide range of social experience, and the processes of historical change, in the manner of Victorian realism.

Bennett moved towards a fiction which centred on the inner life of the characters, isolating Darius in the early episode, and giving his heroine a separate novel, *Hilda Lessways*, in which she re-experiences much of the action of *Clayhanger*, and finds Edwin as mysterious as he found her. Bennett was, however, reluctant to accept entirely the loss of the authoritative, validating voice of traditional realism. He retained a narrative voice external to the characters' consciousness, but the difficulty of locating this voice is evidenced in the frequent use of a curious device which speaks as from a negative point of view. 'Beauty was achieved and none saw it' (Part I, Ch. 1), he says of the Potteries landscape, and of Edwin's Paterian flame, 'it was surprising that no one saw it' (Part I, Ch. 2).

Admitting the non-existence in the community described of any sense of social or historical complexity, he says 'nobody perceived how interesting it was, this interchange of activities, this ebb and flow of money, this sluggish rise and fall of reputations and fortunes, stretching out of one century into another and towards a third!' (Part I, Ch. 3). Throughout *Clayhanger* Bennett keeps insisting that no one perceives a value which he nevertheless describes to us. He is unwilling to confine himself to the isolated impressions of his characters. This negative version of the commentator, the nobody who sees, enables him to retain a suggestion of value which can be externally validated.

Clayhanger, more emphatically than *Anna of the Five Towns* or *The Old Wives Tale* which also employ the 'nobody' device, is a novel in transition between social realism and the modernist exploration of subjectivity. The vestigial mediation by the commentating voice, implied by 'nobody', suggests Bennett's reluctance to recognise the loss of the wider social and historical context, and settle whole-heartedly for his hero's consciousness, as Joyce's *A Portrait of the Artist as a Young Man* was to do a few years later. Like Forster's shifting definition of the pronoun 'we' in *Howards End* (see Chapter 3), Bennett's observing 'nobody' points to the difficulty with which the writers of the Edwardian period relinquished the ideas of authority and community suggested in the authorial voice of Victorian realism. At the same time Bennett, like Forster, admitted uncertainty as to the nature of his readership. His regular column in the *New Age* returned continually to the question of who actually read novels.

NARRATIVES OF PARRICIDE: SYNGE

Clayhanger, with its story of a son rejecting his father's way of life, and its tentative move away from social realism, must be seen in the context of the generational revolt of the new century in which the young repudiated the forms and beliefs by which their fathers had sought to understand society and history. The death of the parent and the release of the child is an exceptionally important episode in the writing of the time. Woolf saw the death of her father, Leslie Stephen, in 1904 as her release into artistic creativity. Years later she noted in her diary:

> Father's birthday. He would have been 96, yes, today; and could have been 96, like other people one has known, but mercifully was not. His life would have entirely ended mine. What would have happened? No writing, no books; – inconceivable.[7]

Clayhanger traces in detail Edwin's exultation in his new feelings of power as his father slides into senility. In *The Old Wives Tale* Sophia 'kills' her father by leaving his sickbed for an assignation. In *Hilda Lessways* Hilda, in similar circumstances, responds too slowly to a telegram announcing her mother's fatal illness. The most famous parricide in the fiction of the period is Paul Morel's killing of his mother in Lawrence's *Sons and Lovers*, 1913. In this case it is the dominant power of the matriarch which must be broken. Mrs Morel's death is a mercy killing, but it releases Paul and gives him a new power and freedom that would have been unattainable had she lived on.

In the same year that *Sons and Lovers* appeared Freud published

Totem and Taboo, his study of parricide, 'this memorable and criminal deed, which was the beginning of so many things – of social organisation, of moral restrictions, and of religion.' [8] Freud's claim that civilisation was founded on parricide, or on guilt over the repressed wish to commit parricide, was little known in England till after the war, but English writers, fascinated by the myth of parricide, were also drawing on nineteenth-century studies of patriarchy and inheritance, and were part of the new century's 'collective Oedipal revolt . . . against the authority of the paternal culture that was their inheritance.' [9]

John Millington Synge's play, *The Playboy of the Western World*, 1907, is the work most explicitly conscious of its parallels with Sophocles's *Oedipus Tyrannus*, and of the social and cultural significance of the myth of parricide. The play celebrates a son's liberation into identity and fulfilment through the fictitious narrative of parricide he tells the community into which he wanders. When he subsequently comes near actual parricide, he is expelled by the now hostile community, and leaves with the father whose master he now is for a greater destiny. Synge recorded in his brief *Autobiography* how it was his reading in youth of Darwin's *The Origin of Species* which released him from religious securities into intellectual and moral exile. 'Incest and parricide were but a consequence of the idea that possessed me . . . I laid a chasm between my present and my past, and between myself and my kindred and friends.' [10] *The Playboy* transforms that supposed parricide into a myth by which the son achieves mastery in the community.

DEFEATED FATHERS: BUTLER, GOSSE, SHAW, BARKER, BARRIE

To Edwardians it was the dead weight of the Victorian inheritance against which they required to assert themselves. A timely model for this assertion was provided in 1903 by the posthumous publication of Samuel Butler's autobiographical novel, *The Way of all Flesh*, written in the 1870s. This revelation of a voice from deep within

Victorianism mocking the sanctity of the family was greatly admired. Shaw praised Butler in the Preface to *Major Barbara*, 1905, as 'the greatest English writer of the latter half of the nineteenth century'.[11]

Butler's novel celebrated a son's successful escape from an oppressive clerical family, and from solemn Victorian ideas of social responsibility, into a purely hedonistic existence. It assaulted all the great institutions of Victorianism: the Church, the family, the public schools and universities, and above all the Victorian paterfamilias, and established the pattern Raymond Williams described for 'the ordinary twentieth-century novel [which] ends with a man going away on his own, having extricated himself from a dominating situation, and found himself in so doing'.[12]

Another influential autobiographical work, Edmund Gosse's *Father and Son*, 1907, recorded a son's struggle against the oppressions of Victorian religion, rather than with materialism and respectability. It described Gosse's early years and conflict with the strict religious principles of his father, the zoologist Philip Gosse. This 'diagnosis of a dying Puritanism' ends with Edmund Gosse's total rejection of his father's beliefs, and brings the narrative to the appropriate conclusion; 'the young man's conscience threw off once for all the yoke of his "dedication", and, as respectfully as he could, without parade or remonstrance, he took a human being's privilege to fashion his inner life for himself.'[13]

Two plays of the period in which idealistic young protagonists struggle with the heavy material burdens they have inherited are Shaw's *Major Barbara* and Harley Granville-Barker's *The Voysey Inheritance*. Both were first performed in 1905; Barker played the part of Barbara's lover, Cusins, in Shaw's play. The plots are comparable; Barbara's femaleness is not an issue in *Major Barbara*. In each play the father is a dynamic, buccaneering Victorian in the manner of the senior Clayhanger, and the offspring is almost overwhelmed in the struggle to assert a separate identity.

Both children have to learn to be buccaneers themselves without sacrificing their moral awareness. Barbara, the Salvation Army officer, sees the advantages of using her father's armaments manufactory as recruiting ground for her faith, and Edward Voysey comes to enjoy using his father's risky business practices to pay back the clients his father swindled. At the end of *The Voysey Inheritance* Edward is told 'You're ten times the man he [his father] ever was.' [14] The line affirms belief in a newly confident younger generation which can learn from their Victorian fathers how to use their instruments of power and their buccaneering methods, but to more principled ends.

The most extravagant dramatic version of the assertive male of the new generation was J. M. Barrie's *Peter Pan*, first performed in 1904, with its picture of the hero as perpetual boy, flying above the money-grubbing, piratical activities of the transformed father-figure, Captain Hook. When the crowing Peter announced 'I'm youth, I'm joy, I'm a little bird that has broken out of the egg', [15] and drove the unmanned Hook overboard into the crocodile's jaws, he voiced the younger generation's hope that they were exorcising the influence of their elders. In Barrie's play, however, the disturbing implications of Peter's rebellion, and of his mythic surname, were very thoroughly contained. Parents taking their children to this popular family play could be reassured both by Peter's insistence that he would always remain a small boy, and by the invariable casting of an adult actress in the role.

FAILED REBELLIONS: GALSWORTHY, FORSTER

The struggle to escape the constraints of a patriarchal society is enacted in the novels of John Galsworthy and E. M. Forster alongside their attempts to find a valid means of expressing that struggle within the confines of Victorian realism. Both writers envisage the possibility of a freer, more liberal existence, but are reluctant to abandon traditional fictional methods. Galsworthy's *The Man of Property*, 1906, was the first volume of the *Forsyte Saga* sequence, the remaining volumes of which were written after World War I. The series finally deteriorated into a celebration of the rituals and securities of prewar English upper middle-class life, and became exemplary of the over-protracted survival of the Victorian social

panoramic novel. But Galsworthy intended *The Man of Property* to
be an indictment of the constraints and oppressions of the patriarchal family, and his failure to realise that aim sprung from his
failure to evolve appropriate narrative methods.

The opening paragraph presents the Forsytes as subjects for
investigation, as exemplary of the patriarchal family as basic social
unit. An observer with 'the gift of psychological analysis' would find
in the Forsytes:

> evidence of that mysterious concrete tenacity which renders a family so
> formidable a unit of society, so clear a reproduction of society in
> miniature. He has been admitted to a vision of the dim roads of social
> progress, has understood something of patriarchal life, of the swarming
> of savage hordes, of the rise and fall of nations.[16]

Galsworthy proposed a scientific enquiry into the phenomenon of
patriarchy, opposing to his array of Victorian fathers and husbands
the figures of the lovers, Irene and Bosinney, who represent the
kinds of culture and vitality excluded from this patriarchal society.

Bosinney, the artistic genius, and the beautiful Irene with her total
commitment to passion, seek to find fulfilment within a society
which forbids such realisation. They cannot be understood within
the world of the Forsytes, and Galsworthy keeps them distanced
from the reader. Their doomed attempt to escape is framed within
the uncomprehending gaze of patriarchal society. The lovers are
never seen alone together, and their meetings are described to us as
glimpsed or imagined by some of the coarsest and most worldly
members of the Forsyte circle. Irene says almost nothing throughout
the novel, in a society which can give no outlet to her feelings.
Bosinney, his revolt against the patriarchs crushed, precipitates
himself silently under a bus.

By keeping his young lovers inarticulate and isolated from the
Forsytes, Galsworthy also isolates them from the reader, and fails to
persuade us of the values that they represent. Lawrence, who began
writing his own family saga, *The Rainbow*, 1915, in this period,
praised *The Man of Property* in an article, 'John Galsworthy', for its
understanding that 'the Forsytes were not full human individuals,
but social beings fallen to a lower level of life'. Lawrence was
unconvinced, however, by the attempt to portray in the lovers the

possibility of a freer, more passionate existence. 'Irene seems to me a sneaking, creeping, spiteful sort of bitch . . . a property mongrel doing dirt in the property kennels.' [17] For Lawrence Galsworthy's failure lay in his inability to escape from the imagining of man as 'social being'. Constrained within Victorian realism, he could recreate to perfection the dead social lives of the patriarchs, but could not truly envisage rebellion.

Galsworthy, like Bennett and Forster, is restless within the confines of realism, but unable to abandon it. His first-paragraph invocation of the psychologically gifted observer who could understand the significance of the Forsytes is an attempt to find some vantage point which will give him authority without requiring him to accept the Forsytes at their own value. As Forster mythologises Howards End, Galsworthy seeks to enhance the status of the lovers with mythologising references to pagan religions, and a world of pastoral eroticism just beyond the glimpse of the Forsytes.

Galsworthy's postwar novels are regressions from the positions of *The Man of Property*. The remaining volumes of the *Forsyte Saga* went soft on the patriarchs; their power had not, after all, been so great. *The Man of Property* was written during the Edwardian agitation for reform of the divorce laws, and ends with Irene trapped in her husband's home, as he slams the door shut on her in a reversal of Nora's celebrated door-slamming exit from her husband's house in Ibsen's *A Doll's House*. In the first sequel, *In Chancery*, 1920, we learn that Irene waited half an hour, quietly left, and got herself a flat and a job teaching music. The irrevocably shut door in retrospect flew open very easily.

E. M. Forster, like Galsworthy, was a would-be escapee from Forsyteism. Both were members of the upper middle class, which gave them their critical insiders' understanding of Forsyteism, and also perhaps their difficulty in escaping the literary tradition associated with it. In each of his Edwardian novels Forster imagined the possibility of escape from a patriarchal society. *Howards End* disintegrates the patriarchal family to replace it with a different kind of family, based on the two Schlegel sisters, in which the 'broken' patriarch has only an invalid existence. The other four novels show individuals struggling to escape the patriarchal tradition, and the community's definition of responsibility and duty, and be true to their own individual values.

In *Where Angels Fear to Tread*, 1905, and *A Room with a View*, 1908, journeys to Italy invoke possibilities of liberation from the constraints of Englishness and middle-classness. In *The Longest Journey*, 1907, and *Maurice*, written in 1913–14 though unpublished till 1971, pastoralism and male friendship offer images of a freer, nobler world outside the confines of bourgeois society and marriage. The initial inspiration for *Maurice* came when Forster visited the socialist Edward Carpenter and his male lover in their rural commune. Carpenter's importance as mentor to Forster and many others, including Lawrence, lay in his rejection of the Victorian concept of manliness. His writings traced the connections between the way in which the manly ethos rejected feeling as appropriate to masculinity, and the oppression of women and the working class by the male ruling class who endorsed that ethos. Carpenter's socialism and his homosexuality were integrated parts of his insistence on the necessity for radical social change, and his rural commune at Millthorpe in Derbyshire exemplified the good life possible outside the confines of patriarchal society.[18]

Maurice was Forster's attempt to realise Carpenter's teachings in a novel. The middle-class hero rejects the constraints of the ruling-class masculine ethos, and escapes with his gamekeeper lover into a world outside class. The escape is admittedly a 'happy ending' in the pastoral mode. Forster said 'I was determined that in fiction anyway two men should fall in love and remain in it for the ever and ever that fiction allows'.[19] Forster was confined not so much by the taboo on his subject matter, as by his commitment to the traditional forms of the novel, and to the world they represented. In his 'Terminal note' of 1960 he spoke with regret of the loss of the prewar England in which he wrote *Maurice*:

> it belongs to an England in which it was still possible to get lost. It belongs to the last moment of the greenwood. *The Longest Journey* belongs there too, and has similarities of atmosphere. Our greenwood ended catastrophically and inevitably. . . . There is no forest or fell to escape to today, no cave in which to curl up, no deserted valley for those who wish neither to reform or corrupt society, but to be left alone.[20]

Forster did not accept Carpenter's insistence on the essential role of political change in the radical rearrangement of personal relations. The personal shift in *Maurice* remained a purely pastoral possibility. Forster in 1960 viewed the world of *Maurice* in softened mood. It was not the constraints of patriarchal society he remembered, but 'the last moment of greenwood'.

NOVELS OF DEPARTURE: LAWRENCE, JOYCE

At the end of this period two of the great writers of modernism produced their own versions of the Edwardian repudiation of inheritance. D. H. Lawrence's third novel, *Sons and Lovers*, ends with a matricide. In this novel it was the mother who represented Victorian ideas of social ambition and respectability, and whose death, therefore, was the necessary prelude to the son's release into full existence. Lawrence had seen the Edwardian novelists' struggle to assert themselves against the past, and criticised the incompleteness of their attempts.

Galsworthy, in Lawrence's account, had understood that men had degenerated into 'social beings' with no existence outside their social roles, but had failed to imagine an alternative. Bennett saw the conditions of English provincial life clearly, but treated them with 'acceptance' and 'resignation'. Wells, indeed, could imagine the possibility of radical change; 'read, *read Tono-Bungay*. It is a great book' Lawrence urged a correspondent. Lawrence, however, found Wells too inclined to linger around the society he had repudiated, 'as a cold and hungry little boy in the street stares at a shop where there is hot pork'.[21] In *Sons and Lovers* he attempted to learn from the half measures of his immediate predecessors, to escape the social being and the patriarchal society which sustained that being, and move to a more open narrative form not centred on 'the old stable ego of the character'.

Paul Morel in *Sons and Lovers* is an artist, but is not seen primarily in that light. Joyce's *A Portrait of the Artist as a Young Man*, 1916, effected that move out of the social world into individual consciousness which Bennett partially achieved with the device of Edwin Clayhanger's aesthetic reveries. Stephen Dedalus escapes from the family, Ireland, the Church, into the impersonality of the artist, in a novel which is totally centred on Stephen's consciousness. In the process Stephen wounds his mother by rejecting her faith, but the parent he has to kill is Ireland, 'the old sow who eats her farrow'.[22] Stephen will recreate Ireland; as he declares in the last paragraph, he will 'forge in the smithy of my soul the uncreated conscience of my race'. To do so he must completely repudiate the Ireland and the family in which he was born.

The *Portrait* marked the emergence of the Edwardian novel of generational revolt into the modern novel. Tentative experiments with rejection of Victorian realism gave way to the full flow of the stream of consciousness. In 1914 the first number of *Blast*, the journal of the Vorticist movement, which included Wyndham Lewis and Ezra Pound, celebrated the escape from circumstance as the necessary condition for the artist. 'The moment a man feels or realises himself as an artist, he ceases to belong to any milieu or time.' [23]

The Edwardians moved in this direction but were reluctant to make a complete break with history. The First World War, which intensified the revolt of the younger generation, rapidly cast those writers who were established literary figures before war broke out as oppressive patriarchs, not always clearly distinguishable from the Victorian ancestors against whom they had rebelled. In literary history this created a division, partly misleading, between the moderns and the Edwardians who shared so many preoccupations.

Chapter 5

New Women and mothers of empire

In Elizabeth Robins's suffragette novel, *The Convert*, 1907, the heroine and her most sympathetic male friend discuss Wells's latest Utopian romance, *In the Days of the Comet*. The friend says, 'Well, he's not my novelist, but it's the keenest intelligence we have applied to fiction.' The heroine replies 'He *is* my novelist. So I've a right to be sorry he knows nothing about women. See here! Even in his most rationalised vision of the New Time, he can't help betraying his old-fashioned prejudice in favour of the "dolly" view of women.'[1]

The discussion points to an anomalous situation. Throughout this period many women were engaged in intensive and much-publicised political activity, but it was male writing about the New Woman and her aspirations which dominated the literary scene. Arguably the women's suffrage movement, and related feminist activities, absorbed female energies which might otherwise have been directed to literary work, and the psychological problems of the women writers who did produce major work in this period (Woolf, Schreiner, Richardson) suggest the difficulties of negotiating a role in the assertively male climate of Edwardian literature.[2]

Women's writing occupied a very marginal position in this decade. The phenomenon of the New Woman had been a major topic for fiction and drama in the 1890s, and, as well as Hardy, Gissing and Shaw, there had been a number of women novelists whose works received attention, including Sarah Grand, Mona Caird and George Egerton.[3] In the Edwardian period the New

Woman remained a major theme, but as the preserve of concerned male writers addressing themselves systematically and scientifically to the subject.

In Virginia Woolf's *The Voyage Out* the heroine feels inhibited by her lover's revelation that he wants to write a book on the fashionable topic of women. 'She felt herself at once singular and under observation' as he explained his idea:

> There it was going on in the background, for all those thousands of years, this curious, silent, unrepresented life. Of course we're always writing about women – abusing them, or jeering at them, or worshipping them; but it's never come from women themselves. I believe we still don't know in the least how they live or what they feel, or what they do precisely.   (Ch. 16)

Terence's conscientious attempts to understand the problem of women are typical of the period. Although it was an age when literature was defined as inherently masculine, the importance of understanding and representing the 'unrepresented life' of women nevertheless engaged many male writers. It is in this context that the women's writing of the period must be understood, and this chapter will look at the male context before turning to the women writers.

WELLS: ANN VERONICA

The male writer who was most concerned with defining women's role was H. G. Wells, and his *Ann Veronica*, 1909, was the major work of the period associated with the topic of the New Woman. The novel's publication provided the occasion for renewed demands for greater censorship of literature by the several literary vigilante groups prominent at the time. (In the case of Joyce's *Dubliners*, publishers' fears of the vigilante groups kept the book unpublished from 1905 to 1914.) *Ann Veronica* was published, but some hostile reviews triggered the Circulating Libraries Association's announcement that it was introducing a new censorship committee to protect its customers against scandalous and immoral works.[4]

The scandal of *Ann Veronica* lay in the heroine's pre-marital sexual activity, and the book was seen as a product of the agitations of the women's movement. The press furore following the publication of the novel somewhat resembled that which had attended Hardy's *Jude the Obscure* in 1895. The unconventional behaviour of the heroine of both books was a target for press abuse, but there was a significant difference between the heroines. Sue Bridehead in *Jude the Obscure* was pre-eminently a mother of the era of the Decadents, encouraging suicidal tendencies in her infant charges. Ann Veronica was proposed as the perfect mother for an improved race.

In the 1890s the Decadents and the New Women were viewed as twin threats to the future of the race.[5] An increasingly publicised panic built up in the last years of the nineteenth century as a result of the decline observed in the birthrate from the 1870s on, a decline which was seen as closely associated with the agitation for women's rights. With this went fears about the unhealthiness of the race which was being produced in the great cities, fears which were intensified at the turn of the century by the medical reports on recruits for the Boer War.[6] Sue Bridehead, rearing children who hanged each other on pegs around the wall, fulfilled the gloomiest speculations about the New Woman's role in this racial decline.

Ann Veronica broke this link between the New Woman and Decadence, with the story of an independent young woman, of great physical and intellectual superiority, who resists parental and social pressure and selects for herself the best mate with whom to produce an improved race. The novel was written in the context of the eugenics movement which was at its height in this period. This movement stressed the need for the introduction of state policies to encourage citizens to exercise greater responsibility in matters of sexual selection, and to facilitate the breeding of an improved race. Wells's attitude to these ideas was ambivalent. His science-fiction romance, *The Time-Machine*, 1895, showed the future consequences of unplanned breeding, but his 1903 Utopian speculation, *Mankind in the Making*, was scornful about the possibilities of achieving planned selective breeding by the bureaucratic methods favoured by the eugenicists.[7]

What he urged in *Ann Veronica* was the need for gifted individuals to find appropriate mates uninhibited by social restrictions which were themselves contributing to racial decline. In another Utopian speculation, *A Modern Utopia*, 1905, Wells insisted that 'the supreme and significant expression of individuality should lie in the selection of a partner for procreation.'[8] *Ann Veronica* is organised around this 'supreme expression'; the purpose of Ann's feminist activities is to bring her to the realisation of this point. In this Wells was running counter to the main line of the eugenics movement, which saw the subjection of women as a necessary part of successful planned breeding.[9]

In handing the power of sexual selection to the individual woman, however, Wells could cite Darwin who, in *The Descent of Man*, had described the existence and effect of female sexual selection in some tribes:

> Preference on the part of the women, steadily acting in any one direction, would ultimately affect the character of the tribe; for the women would generally choose not merely the handsomest men . . . but those who were at the same time best able to defend and support them. Such well-endowed pairs would commonly rear a larger number of offspring than the less favoured.[10]

Ann Veronica took up Darwin's suggestion that female selection might advantageously be exercised in cases where social conditions would otherwise force women to accept husbands who were old or in some way physically unfit. Ann resists social pressures, and selects a socially inappropriate, but otherwise supremely fit, mate.

Ann Veronica is thus the story of a young woman's struggle to realise her biological destiny and resist the diversions a decadent society puts in her way. Her intellectual superiority is demonstrated by her biological studies, her strong physique by the vigour with which she fights off a would-be seducer. She turns down the man her father chooses to be her husband, a boneheaded devotee of Ruskin who worships women as 'queens'; and she resists the bourgeois would-be adulterer who tries to seduce her to the strains of *Tristan and Isolde*.

Her attempts to identify with the Fabians, and then with the suffragettes, are seen as understandable diversions from her real, but as yet unrecognised, purpose. The misdirected robustness of the suffragette leader, Kitty Brett, a sketch of Christabel Pankhurst, further emphasises the diversionary nature of the movement. In prison Ann realises her destiny.

> A woman wants a proper alliance with a man, a man who is better stuff than herself. . . . She wants to be free – she wants to be legally and economically free, so as not to be subject to the wrong man: but only God who made the world, can alter things to prevent her being slave to the right one.[11]

When she eventually proposes alliance to her tutor, Capes, her appropriate mate, he exclaims in comic role reversal 'this is very sudden' (Ch. 14).

The subsequent passages, in which Wells describes the defiant runaway liaison of Ann and Capes, are the weakest in the book. Wells was seeking to evolve a method of writing about sexual relations more freely and responsively than Victorian constraints had allowed. What he achieved was accurately indicated by Rebecca West, in an article, 'Uncle Bennett', which described the work of the Edwardians as avuncular and old fashioned:

> The only thing against Uncle Wells was that he did so love to shut himself up in the drawing-room and put out all the lights except the lamp with the pink silk shade, and sit down at the piano and have a lovely time warbling in too fruity a tenor, to the accompaniment of chords struck draggingly with the soft pedal held down, songs of equal merit to 'The Rosary'.[12]

The novel does, however, have passages which show considerable empathy with the heroine, notably in Chapter 5 when Ann is being pursued through London by a man who wants to pick her up. Wells is also wryly aware of his own role as a representer of the women's cause, as when the silliest of the suffragettes gushes about the great male minds sympathetic to the cause, including 'Wilkins the author' (Ch. 7).

The conclusion shows Ann, about to become a mother, reconciled with her estranged father. This was essential to Wells's purpose in affirming his heroine's readiness to take her place in the continuing tradition of humanity. She now accepts that 'the great time is over, and I have to go carefully and bear children' (Ch. 17), but in the terms of the book she has already passed the supreme test of individuality. It was not the book's purpose to be attentive to Ann's consciousness; she was studied for her role in the evolving history of the human race.

In the novel, *The New Machiavelli*, 1911, Wells's politician hero builds his career on an 'attempt to graft the Endowment of Motherhood in some form or other upon British Imperialism'. He is swept into Parliament and 'benches of Imperialists cheered me on my way to the table between the whips' (Part III, Ch. 4). (This is partly ironic as a sex scandal will shortly condemn him to political oblivion.) State provision of financial support for mothers was a Fabian scheme in this period and related to the general concern about the degeneracy of the race. Imperialism and socialism met in worries about the need for race improvement, as London's *The People of the Abyss* suggested (see Chapter 3). Socialist concern for the human race easily shaded into imperialist concern for the English race, and Wells's hero's attempts to 'biologise Imperialism' show how easily concern for the New Woman could become concern for the mothers of empire.

THE CONTEXT OF MALE WRITING: SHAW, BENNETT, LAWRENCE

In 1903 the play *Man and Superman* by Wells's colleague in socialism, Shaw, adopted the contemporary emphasis on the New Woman as mother rather than wife.[13] Shaw anticipated Wells in presenting his heroine, another Ann, as a woman whose determination to take the sexual initiative will help save democracy from the dangers of ill breeding. Ann, 'one of the vital geniuses',[14] is seeking a father for the Superman but, instinctively realising she must conceal her purposes, she adopts the stereotype Victorian role of the helpless female in need of male protection. This necessary inarticulacy on Ann's part dictates that Tanner, the intellectual whom she has marked down as her prey, must spend the play explaining her strategies to her, and to the audience. The comedy lies in his failure to realise that he himself is her destined victim. *Man and*

Superman is thus organised around a recurrent theme of the decade, the articulation by men to women of women's situation.

Another male attempt to articulate women's situation was Arnold Bennett's *Hilda Lessways*, 1911, which Bennett intended to be the first systematic study in fiction of the ways in which women differ from men.

> I had a goodish large notion for the Hilda book – of portraying the droves of the whole sex, instead of whole masculine droves. I think I can do something with this, showing the multitudinous activities of the whole sex, the point of view of the whole sex, against a mere background of masculinity. I had a sudden vision of it. It has never been done.[15]

His qualifications for writing the study included several years in the 1890s working as deputy editor and then editor of the journal *Woman*, (no relation to the current journal). In this role he not only advised his female contributors and revised their work, but wrote much of the journal himself under various female pseudonyms, adopting personae appropriate to the topic. This experience of multiple cross-dressing presumably contributed to his eagerness to rewrite the story he had already told in *Clayhanger* from the different point of view of the heroine, Hilda, who, in the earlier book, is presented as a figure of mystery.

Bennett's journals document the difficulties he experienced in presenting Hilda:

> I didn't seem to be getting near to the personality of Hilda in my novel. You scarcely ever do get near a personality. There is a tremendous lot to do in fiction that no-one has yet done. When M [Marguerite Bennett, née Soulié] comes downstairs from the attic, in the middle of some house arrangement, and asks me if such and such a thing will do, and runs up again excited – why? And the mood of the servant as, first thing in the morning, she goes placidly round the house opening the shutters. The fact is, the novelist seldom really *penetrates*. (Vol. I, 373)

Woolf, in her criticism of Bennett, used *Hilda Lessways* as an example of his failure to catch the essence of his characters. Bennett's *Journals*, however, voice worries about characterisation rather similar to Woolf's; certainly, like Terence in *The Voyage Out*, he wants to record the 'unrepresented life' of women.

Woolf also saw violence and aggression in Bennett's attempts to seize character, qualities exemplified in the passage above. Like Kipling's Kim entering the soul of the East (see Chapter 2), he was determined to know his female characters. This insistence suggests the comparison between women and colonised races so often found in writing of this period. Other passages describe a male imperialist resistance to any encroachment on the self.

> I do not like to think that I am dependent spiritually, to even a slight degree, on anyone. I do not like to think that I am not absolutely complete and sufficient in myself to myself. I could not ask for a caress, except as a matter of form, and to save the *amour-propre* of her who I know was anxious to confer it.   (Vol. I, 293)

Bennett's *Journals* reveal conscientious attempts to research his female characters, recording interviews with women of various ages and social groups. *Hilda Lessways* was to be the main product of this research. The voice which describes Hilda in this book is quite distinct from that which describes Edwin in *Clayhanger*. It is the voice of an intelligent man of the world who has attempted to come to terms with the problem of women. 'She is not to be comprehended on an acquaintance of three days. Years must go to the understanding of her.'[16] This connoisseur's tone is heightened in the passage which describes the excitement of Hilda and her friend at the plight of an indigent spinster. 'They were fine, they were touching – but they were also rather deliciously amusing' (Part I, Ch. 8). The reader is invited to respond as a seasoned connoisseur of the woman as aesthetic object.

The revelation, in *Hilda Lessways*, of what lay behind Hilda's mystery in *Clayhanger* emphasises particularly her apparent intellectual superiority. Her defence for Victor Hugo, which so impressed Edwin, turns out to be based on a sentimental attachment to one poem read in childhood. The knowledge of the history of printing which she also flaunts was read up specifically to impress him. It is true that in this sequel we are given Hilda's sense of Edwin as mysterious, but her idea of him as 'subtle, baffling and benevolent, and above all superior' (Part II, Ch. 3) does not significantly contradict what we were told about him in the previous book, and serves rather to enhance his status. Hilda's apparent superiority, however, is dissipated as Bennett analyses the species of women scientifically.

Another work begun in this period is D. H. Lawrence's *The Lost Girl*, published in 1920 but partly drafted under the title *The Insurrection of Miss Houghton* in 1912. This work, Lawrence's most 'Edwardian' novel, begins by proposing to examine the national problem of the 'odd women', the surplus of unmarried middle-class women. The 'scientific' concern, with which the novel begins, relates to the debates of the Edwardian period; the book was partly intended as a critical response to Bennett's *Anna of the Five Towns*, as well as owing an obvious debt to Wells.[17]

FEMINIST WRITERS: ROBINS, SCHREINER

The women's writing of the Edwardian period must be seen in this context of male writing which sought to understand the problem of woman and explain it to her. The intensive political activity is little recorded in fiction. The major suffragette novel was Elizabeth Robins's *The Convert*, produced successfully as a play, *Votes for Women*, in the same year, 1907. Robins was an actress, best known for her playing of Ibsen roles, notably the New Woman heroines, Hilde Wangel in *The Master-Builder*, and Rebecca West in *Rosmersholm*. Shaw commented on 'that devastating stage pathos which is Miss Robins's most formidable professional speciality'.[18] She became the first president of the Women Writers Suffrage League, founded in 1908.

The central situation of both play and novel draws on melodrama, and on the plot of Henry James's anti-feminist novel *The Bostonians*, 1886. The main characters are a rising star of the Tory Shadow Cabinet, his innocent young fiancée, and an older woman, his ex-lover, who has become a charismatic leader of the women's movement, and who threatens to turn the fiancée into the 'new Joan of Arc' of women's suffrage, unless the politician declares his support for the cause in the forthcoming election campaign.

The book derives its strength from the fact that Robins had an actress's eye for the importance of performance in political and social life, and for the relations between material, performer and audience. The novel contrasts two worlds, the country house, and the streets where the women are demonstrating. In one world a drawing-room comedy is acted out; well-known, much-rehearsed roles are played to perfection, especially by the female performers. 'She knew with an absolute precision just how perfectly at that moment she herself was presenting the average man's picture of the ideal type of reposeful womanhood' (Vol. I, Ch. 5). The other world is street-theatre where the performers are still seeking viable roles. There is a strong contrast between the polished but dead theatre of polite society, and the dynamic and unpredictable theatre of the street.

The novel resembles Tressell's *The Ragged Trousered Philanthropists* in its extensive treatment of the problems of recalcitrant audiences. Both novels are polemical, and incorporate political content for the reader in the form of long orations by the characters; both make the reactions of the audiences within the story an integral part of that content. Robins's female characters seek to become public speakers and have to tackle the difficulty of creating appropriate roles.

They succeed best where there is a possibility of adapting existing stereotypes; the book insists that women can work only within the framework of roles already understood by the public. Ernestine, the most successful performer, adopts a provocative soubrette persona; another activist, who comes on like 'an overblown Adelphi heroine' (Vol. I, Ch. 7), attracts enthusiastic audiences. The most startling failure is a drawing-room vamp whose well-attested sex appeal loses all effect in the street. The novel recognises the class nature of audiences. The heroine, accustomed to West End theatre, cannot understand the appeal of a particularly successful working-class speaker, 'having no key either to her pathos or her power' (Vol. I, Ch. 7).

Robins's awareness of the public/theatrical roles available for women, including their class content, breaks down only once. She allows to her heroine, Vida, a natural eloquence, unexplained by experience, training or readiness to adapt existing roles in the repertoire. It is Vida who links women's situation to the imperialist nature of the British state, explaining it as another form of colonial domination (Vol. I, Ch. 10). Robins's problem here was that there was no existing theatrical tradition within which Vida could make her claim that women must find new parts to play which will break down the imperial structures of British society. At this point Robins's shrewd insistence on the advantages of working within the repertoire becomes a handicap.

The relation between the women's movement and the need to change an imperialist, militarist state is the subject also of Olive Schreiner's *Women and Labour*, 1911. Schreiner, whose major novel, *The Story of an African Farm*, had appeared in 1883, produced little in the Edwardian period. She offered an explanation in her preface; most of the manuscript of this book, intended to be her masterwork, had been burned when the British army looted her Johannesburg home during the Boer War, and she had spent the decade reconstructing it. This explanation has been much disputed, but the story of the fragmentary and precarious survival of a feminist text, nearly destroyed in an imperialist war, seems appropriately emblematic of how women writers viewed their work in this period.[19]

Schreiner's notion that if women played a greater political role it would shift the state away from its militarist preoccupations is based on women's role as mothers; those who supply the 'primal munition' for war will be more careful in its use. The book laments the lack of a significant role for women, either as worker or mother, in contemporary life, and details the varieties of 'female parasitism'. These include the writing of popular fiction:

> Even in the little third-rate novelist whose works cumber the ground, we see often a pathetic figure, when we recognise that beneath that failure in a complex and difficult art, may lie buried a sound legislator, an able architect, an original scientific investigator, or a good judge. . . . Both the creative writer and the typist, in their respective spheres, are merely finding outlets for their powers in the direction of least resistance.[20]

Schreiner's line-of-least-resistance argument was an explanation of a phenomenon embarrassing to feminists, the dominance of the mass readership for fiction by such sentimental and politically reactionary writers of romance as Marie Corelli and Baroness Orczy and their many imitators.

WOMAN AS CHILD: CHILDREN'S FICTION, MANSFIELD

Another line of least resistance was that of children's fiction in which the presence of female contributors was clearly unexceptionable. Within the confines of this genre women writers could explore their situation without drawing hostile attention. The best-known Edwardian women writers in this genre were Frances Hodgson Burnett and Edith Nesbit. Most of the appeal of Burnett's *The Secret Garden*, 1911, despite its concluding reinstatement of the squirearchy, lies in its exploration of the heroine's discovery of a space of her own. The socialist Nesbit's series of children's novels in this decade included *The Amulet*, 1905, in which her time-travelling children visit, among other places, a future Utopia, where their guide is a discontented small boy, named Wells after the thinker whose teachings inspired the society.

Nesbit used her child heroes to criticise the existing society. Julia Briggs suggests in her biography, 1987, that

> something within her clearly responded and corresponded to the position of the child in her society. . . . She experienced all the child's primitive desires to control the world around her, yet she was conscious, as the children in her books are, of being a subject in a world where the rules are laid down by full-grown men – and where women, like children, are relegated to marginal positions and occupations.[21]

In her children's discontents, and in the shifting roles of her girls and boys, Nesbit questioned the feminine identity offered adult women, and the assumption that little girls move easily into feminine roles.

The emphasis on the ambiguities in the transition from child to woman is a major theme of the period in fiction generally. The best of Katherine Mansfield's early short stories, written in this period, centre on children. 'Are you a child, or are you playing at being one?' the teenage waitress in the story 'At Lehmann's', 1911, is asked by a lecherous customer. It is a difficult question to answer in a patriarchal society, and reverberates throughout Mansfield's early work. Two early stories, 'How Pearl Button was Kidnapped', 1910, and 'The Little Girl', 1912, are set within the consciousness of very small girls and in fairy-tale form. The later story recalls 'Red Riding Hood' when the frightened child, forced in her grandmother's absence to seek refuge with the wolf-father, recognises his dual aspect as threat and protection. 'What a big heart you've got, father dear.'[22]

D. H. Lawrence used Mansfield as a model for Gudrun in *Women in Love*, 1920, where Gudrun's talent for the miniature in her sculpturing becomes a comment on her destructive tendencies. Mansfield is a rare example of a writer exclusively associated with the short story, and the brevity and relative marginality of this still, in English, fairly new form offered her a refuge analogous to that of children's fiction. Widespread knowledge of Chekhov's work, and an ensuing rise in status for the short story, came after World War I.

Mansfield's first short story, 'The Tiredness of Rosabel', written in 1908 though first published in the collection, *Something Childish and Other Stories*, 1924, examines the uncertain transition from childhood to womanhood, and the nature of the fictional forms available to the female imagination. The story realises the imaginative life of an overworked, teenage, millinery assistant, who builds a romantic fantasy around a male customer. The subject is the same as that of Henry James's novella, *In the Cage*, 1898, but, where James emphasised the triumphant ability of the creative imagination to construct from negligible material, Mansfield is concerned with the contamination of the female imagination by the meretricious romantic fantasies available to the socialised woman. In Rosabel, the authentically powerful imagination typical of Mansfield's children is being channelled into hackneyed romantic forms, which divert her justifiable class and gender resentments into the fantasy of a doubly impossible lover who is both aristocratic and understanding.

Mansfield's first published collection of stories was *In a German Pension*, 1911; she later regretted setting her stories of a brutal patriarchy and its acquiescent female subjects in Germany. In 1914, when the location of the stories made their sentiments acceptable to the British public, she refused to allow them to be republished. The best stories suggest the problem of the transition from child to woman in a patriarchal society. 'At Lehmann's' is about a young waitress, whose juvenile looks are a commercial asset to the café owner, who has exiled his pregnant wife to the upstairs rooms. The waitress builds a romantic fantasy around a male customer which may shortly exile her in a similar way. In 'The Child-who-was-Tired' the child-slavey's fantasies become murderous as the tension between her adult responsibilities and her childish dreams becomes too much. In the last sentence she retreats into the only identity left to her, a dream of walking through monochrome uninhabited landscape, 'a little white road with tall black trees on either side, a little road that led to nowhere, and where nobody walked at all – nobody at all' (p. 766).

FEMALE CONSCIOUSNESS: RICHARDSON, WOOLF

Dorothy Richardson, like Katherine Mansfield a woman writer associated with modernism, began writing her stream-of consciousness series, *Pilgrimage*, in this period; the first novel, *Pointed Roofs*, appeared in 1915. Like Mansfield with the short story, she is seeking a narrative form not already strongly associated with male writers. In her foreword she described how she began writing by 'attempting to produce a feminine equivalent of the current masculine realism', at a time when 'realism was synonymous with Arnold Bennett'.[23]

Richardson's heroine, Miriam, is beset by men anxious to define for her the kind of writing women should produce. In the second novel in the series, *Backwater*, 1916, a male friend urges Miriam to write fiction on the lines of a recent model, the revealing title of which is *Confessions of a Woman*. In the later volumes, written after World War I, but continuing to depict the Edwardian period, Miriam argues frequently with a novelist called Hypo Wilson, modelled on Wells, who insists that women's writing should concentrate on the emotional life. In the late *Dawn's Left Hand*,

1931, Richardson rewrites a version of the seduction scene in *Ann Veronica*.

Richardson's solution to her search for an alternative to male realism is total immersion in the consciousness of Miriam. The phrase 'stream of consciousness' was first used by the novelist May Sinclair in a 1918 review of Richardson's novels:

> Nothing happens. It is just life going on and on. It is Miriam Henderson's stream of consciousness going on and on. . . . In identifying herself with this life, which is Miriam's stream of consciousness, Miss Richardson produces her effect of being the first, of getting closer to reality than any of our novelists who are trying so desperately to get close. No attitude or gesture of her own is allowed to come between her and her effect. . . . It is as if no other writers had ever used their senses so purely and with so intense a joy in their use. This intensity is the effect of an extreme concentration on the thing seen and felt.[24]

In *Pointed Roofs* the method of total immersion in Miriam's consciousness is at one with the theme of Miriam's struggle for greater expressiveness as she journeys from her home to work as a teacher in Germany. Already repressed by the female role-playing required of her, she is further constrained by her Englishness, 'the familiar feeling of English self-consciousness'. The absorption of the pupils in their music becomes a model to her; 'these girls were learning in Germany not to be afraid of "playing with expression" ' (Ch. 3).

As Sinclair suggested the narrative concentrates on Miriam's sensuous registration of the world around her; it is an extreme example of how to burn with a Paterian flame. Applying thoroughly Pater's injunction 'to discriminate every moment some passionate attitude in those about us', Richardson, as Elaine Showalter complains, 'would not discriminate among her experiences.'[25] This comprehensive responsiveness was seen as characteristic of general fictional directions. When Edward Garnett accepted *Pointed Roofs* for publication he described it as 'female Impressionism'.[26] Impressionism was the term used to describe the major shift in fiction and poetry from the object perceived to the effect produced (see Chapters 6 and 7).

Richardson, however, saw the stream of consciousness as a

distinctively female method of writing. In her Edwardian revolt against the traditional realist concept of a stable identity, she characterised that identity as male. 'I' is always masculine to Richardson, a theme Woolf was to reiterate in the last chapter of *A Room of One's Own*. Sinclair, in her review, agreed in seeing Richardson's method as distinctively feminine in its complete avoidance of the authoritative authorial voice. 'She must not tell a story, or handle a situation, or set a scene; she must avoid drama as she avoids narrative. And there are some things she must not be. She must not be the wise all-knowing author. She must be Miriam Henderson' (p. 58).

Woolf, in a famous review, declared that Richardson had 'invented . . . a sentence which we might call the psychological sentence of the female gender . . . in order that it may descend to the depths and investigate the crannies of Miriam Henderson's consciousness.'[27] Woolf's controversial claims for a distinctively female sentence are ambiguously endorsed by Richardson in her foreword of 1938, which described 'feminine prose . . . unpunctuated, moving from point to point without formal obstruction' (p. 12). She pointed to the use of the stream-of-consciousness method by male writers such as Joyce and Proust, but was anxious to deny the allegation that the method originated with Henry James, 'a charmed and charming high priest of nearly all the orthodoxies, inhabiting a softly lit enclosure he mistook until 1914 for the universe' (p. 11). Richardson saw her experiment as part of the struggle to escape from the forms of realism which she defined as male.

Woolf's *The Voyage Out* was drafted at least five times between 1908 and 1913, and a breakdown in 1913 delayed publication until 1915. Her difficulties were an intensified version of Schreiner's and Richardson's difficulties in writing in this period. The novel is a comprehensive account of a young woman confronting the existing tradition and her need to find her own place in it. Where Robins's heroine demanded full participation in the male-dominated world and Richardson's luxuriated in a distinctively female vision, Woolf's Rachel is entirely daunted.

The structure and imagery of *The Voyage Out* evoke *Heart of Darkness*. As in *Heart of Darkness*, the men who set out on the voyage

see themselves as figures of enlightenment, but women are specifically included among those to be enlightened; 'few things at the
present time mattered more than the enlightenment of women' (Ch.
12). Rachel's position on the journey is therefore anomalous; it is
revealed in detail that civilisation does not belong to her. She is
among the objects of male imperialism, under-educated and
inarticulate, oppressed by the books which represent civilisation.

Early in the book Rachel, eager to understand her elders, looks
through *Who's Who* and resolves to be herself in spite of the weighty
tradition revealed there. (Woolf's own identity as daughter of Leslie
Stephen, the first editor of the *Dictionary of National Biography*, is
evoked here.) Later she is first exhilarated and then intimidated by
Gibbon's *The Decline and Fall of the Roman Empire*. Immediately
before her fatal illness she is silently questioning her fiancé's
interpretation of Milton. In this majestic tradition the slim part which
a woman can play is represented by Jane Austen, praised by the
politician Dalloway because 'she does not attempt to write like a man'
(Ch. 4); he then falls asleep while *Persuasion* is read aloud to him.

Rachel has to contend not only with the weight of tradition, but
with the anxiety of her fiancé and his friend to understand women,
enlighten them, and write books interpreting women's problems to
women readers. The ambitions of the European male of the period
to civilise women and other inferior races, and to scientifically
understand them, is here observed by one of the colonised. The
episode of Rachel's reading Gibbon marks a crucial stage in her
realisation of the difficulties of constructing a female identity for
herself. She initially feels liberated from herself by the language, by
the way in which the words 'seemed to drive roads back to the very
beginning of the world' (Ch. 13), but the image of those roads of
civilisation recalls the patriarchies which built them, and her own
place in the order, indicated by her growing awareness of her love
for Terence.

This awareness reaches crisis in the journey back along those
roads of civilisation to the jungle from which they emerged. When
Terence and Rachel articulate their love, she parodies the reiteration
of Conrad's Kurtz, murmuring 'Terrible – terrible' (Ch. 20). This is
the moment which confronts her with the abyss which Kurtz saw,

and forces her to define her life. By dying shortly afterwards, Rachel tacitly affirms her recognition of the impossible strength of the patriarchal tradition, and rejects the place as a mother for empire so persistently offered by the male writers of the period, and their representatives within the novel. Her death is a refusal of the femininity she must otherwise assume. In killing her heroine Woolf completed a novel which was the period's sharpest attack on the contemporary male as enlightened colonist.

Chapter 6

Poems, audiences and anthologies

One of the last remarks Hardy is recorded as making is that 'his only ambition, so far as he could remember, was to have some poem or poems in a good anthology like the *Golden Treasury*.'[1] If the remark was characteristic of the writer who titled one of his last poems 'He Never Expected Much', it was also appropriate coming from a poet who established his poetic reputation in the Edwardian period. Hardy published his first four volumes of poems and the poetic drama, *The Dynasts*, in the years from 1898 to 1914. It was a period when a poet's consciousness of his place in the English literary tradition might well include his representation in the right anthologies.

The Edwardian period may be seen as bounded by two anthologies, the first edition of *The Oxford Book of English Verse*, 1900, by Sir Arthur Quiller-Couch, and *Georgian Poetry 1911–1912*, 1912, edited by Edward Marsh. The *Oxford Book* represented the great tradition of English verse up to that date, replacing the *Golden Treasury* as the premier anthology. Hardy, whose first collection of poems, *Wessex Poems*, was published in 1898, did not make it into this edition. When a second edition, taking the tradition up to 1918, was eventually published in 1939, the first Hardy entry was 'The Darkling Thrush'. This poem, published in the *Graphic* at the end of the century to commemorate that end, is a definitive anthology piece, and clearly written to be such.[2] It is not dissimilar, in its judicious balance of warning and affirmation, to Kipling's 'Recessional', 1897, one of the last-written poems to make it into the original *Oxford Book*. With 'The Darkling Thrush' Hardy, who wrote so much of other kinds of poem in this period, was demonstrating that he could also place himself in the line of anthologised English poets.

The title *Georgian Poetry 1911–1912* was a statement of belief in a newly invigorated school of poetry. One of the contributors, Lawrence, reviewed the volume, and described the new spirit of liberation it represented after the 'years of demolition' that had gone before. Novelists such as Hardy had demolished the old system of beliefs and made a renascence in poetry possible.[3] Unlike another influential contemporary anthology, *Des Imagistes*, 1914, edited by Ezra Pound and announcing an internationalist school of modern poetry, *Georgian Poetry 1911–1912* was distinctively English. The Georgians were anxious to dissociate themselves from the Edwardians, but it was still very specifically an English tradition that they saw themselves recreating.

The *Oxford Book* affirmed and consolidated tradition; the Georgian poets, in opposition, insisted they were building on the ruins. Another issue was raised by Ford Madox Ford in 1911, when he confessed that, like most of his contemporaries, he had read no poetry since he left school. Only the professional necessity of reading, as editor, poems submitted to *The English Review*, had caused him to resume the habit.[4] Ford's claim was clearly made for effect, and prefaced a volume of his own poems, but the question 'Who reads poetry?' was central to the period.

The main audience of any size was in the schoolroom. As the study of English literature came to be seen as central to the inculcation of awareness of the national spirit, anthologies which demonstrated the national tradition assumed importance. The *Oxford Book* and the *Golden Treasury* covered the mainstream tradition of English poetry, but the kind of poetry thought especially appropriate for schoolrooms was exemplified by the anthology, *Lyra Heroica*, 1892, edited by W. E. Henley, which was frequently reprinted in this period. Henley's selection covered the previous five centuries but, while the choices from earlier centuries included some love-poems and elegies, those from the nineteenth century were unremittingly martial or patriotic. The selection and chronological ordering irresistibly suggested that, while earlier Englishmen might have had leisure to pluck myrtles or go a-maying, the current breed was made of altogether sterner stuff.

One of the most active and influential members of the English Association, founded in 1907 to oversee the role of English in the national education, was Sir Henry Newbolt, whose late 1890s poems, 'Vitai Lampada' and 'Drake's Drum', were among the most famous examples of the kind of English imperialist verse circulated in schoolroom anthologies.[5] The major imperialist poet was Kipling, but according to Wells, his influence as a dynamic force among even the socialist-minded young peaked in 1897 with 'Recessional'.[6] This poem was part of the 'invention of tradition' of the period, a hymn attending the ceremonials of empire, and affirming the place of verse as an integral part of the imperialist tradition.

In the next decade, however, the influence of 'Recessional' was countered by that of Housman's *A Shropshire Lad*, 1896. George Orwell claimed that by 1910 'the writer who had the deepest hold upon the thinking young was almost certainly Housman', and that Housman's pastoralism and scepticism appealed to young readers revolting against Church and Empire.[7] *A Shropshire Lad* offered an alternative tradition, but one, as Orwell pointed out, which was also self-consciously masculine, to the juvenile audience brought up on *Lyra Heroica* and Kipling. It was an offer taken up by the Georgian poets.

Ford, describing the schoolroom as the place where poetry reading stopped for most people, blamed the usual scapegoats, the Victorians. Tennyson and his contemporaries had given him a disgust for poetry's pretentiousness at school. He made exceptions, however, for the 'still, small, private voice' of Christina Rossetti, and for those late Victorians, Hardy and Yeats.[8] This comment points to a central anomaly of the Edwardian period, that the major poetry was produced by two Victorians widely supposed to have already done their best work before the century opened. Lawrence, a warm admirer of Hardy, placed him among the demolitionists. Pound, a warm admirer of Yeats, suggested in 1914 that Yeats's Irish balladry had already brought about a late Victorian revolution, and that no one could be expected to run a second revolution.[9] Both Yeats and Hardy, however, persisted in seeking a new post-Victorian identity.

HARDY: *POEMS OF 1912-1913* AND OTHERS

Hardy made a late public entrance as a poet, with *Wessex Poems*, 1898, and published three more collections before the First World War, *Poems of the Past and the Present*, 1901, *Time's Laughingstocks*, 1909, and *Satires of Circumstance*, 1914. Poems written much earlier in his life made up a substantial part of the first and third of the four volumes, but the majority of the poems published in this period were of recent date. In 1897, two years after the hostile reception of *Jude the Obscure*, he noted 'Perhaps I can express more fully in verse ideas and emotions which run counter to the inert crystallised opinion – hard as a rock – which the vast body of men have vested interests in supporting. . . . If Galileo had said in verse that the world moved, the Inquisition might have let him alone.'[10]

For the rest of his life he became a poet, and his prefaces insist on the unsystematic and occasional nature of his poems. *Poems of the Past and the Present* is

> a series of feelings and fancies written down in widely differing moods and circumstances, and at various dates; it will probably be found therefore to possess little cohesion of thought or harmony of colouring. I do not greatly regret this. Unadjusted impressions have their value.[11]

This insistence on 'mere impressions of the moment', (General Preface of 1911), was long-standing with Hardy. In 1886, after visiting an exhibition of Impressionist art he had noted that this was the direction for literature;

> what you carry away with you from a scene is the true feature to grasp; or in other words, *what appeals to your own individual eye and heart in particular* amid much that does not so appeal, and which you therefore omit to record.[12]

Hardy was here anticipating Ford's later descriptions of Impressionism as the major literary shift of the new century. Ford's 1914 essay, 'On Impressionism', described the outmoded literature of 'non-Impressionism . . . an attempt to gather together the opinions of as many reputable persons as may be, and to render them truthfully and without exaggeration.' In contrast the new literature was 'the record of the impression of a moment; it is not a sort of rounded, annotated record of a set of circumstances – it is the record of the recollection in your mind of a set of circumstances that happened ten years ago – or ten minutes.' Ford added that Impressionism recognised that 'we are almost always in one place with our minds somewhere quite other.'[13]

Hardy's *Poems of 1912–1913*, published in *Satires of Circumstance*, were his supreme example of poetry as a record of impressions. In the twenty-one poems of the series, which along with some related poems elsewhere in the volume, were a response to the death of his long-estranged wife, Emma, Hardy was reacting to her own record of their relationship which he read in the manuscript *Some Recollections*, and to her home county, Cornwall, where they had courted, and which he revisited. These responses to Emma's memories, and to the revisited landscapes of Cornwall, explore the shifting and uncertain status of the memories and impressions which impose themselves on Hardy.

Hardy in his *Life* spoke of those who, like himself, came to poetry late in life after 'its outspringing may have been frozen and delayed for half a lifetime', and of his own 'faculty . . . for burying an emotion in my heart or brain for forty years, and exhuming it at the end of that time as fresh as when interred'.[14] In *Poems of 1912–1913* his personal inheritance of disinterred memory forced the poetry of mere impressions to its highest intensity. The memories evoked by Cornwall and by Emma's record are heightened from fugitive impressions, of dubious status but intense personal significance, to be reproduced semi-tangibly as ghosts. The hauntings of the poems are always realised as the product of disinterred memory under intense emotional pressure; there is no implication of some general supernatural system as there is increasingly in Yeats's poetry at this time.

The memories attain such hallucinatory intensity that they appear as ghosts in the poems; in 'After a Journey', the poem to which

Emma's memories in *Some Recollections* contributed most, her apparent physical presence is registered in 'your nut-coloured hair/ And gray eyes, and rose flush coming and going'. In 'At Castle Boterel' Emma and Hardy's past figures are distinct on the wet road behind the waggonnette in which the present Hardy travels. These vivid sense impressions undermine our conviction in the existence of the boundary between subjective and objective reality. Even the geography of Cornwall, alien within the poems, undermines his, and our, grasp on reality. In 'A Dream or No' the poet of Wessex questions the external reality of the landscapes of Cornwall. 'Does there even a place like Saint-Juliot exist?'

The hauntings suggest to Hardy the remote possibility of remedying what the poems lament, the failure of communication between the Hardys. In the first poem of the series, 'The Going', the 'you' to whom the poem is addressed becomes a 'she' who was geographically alien. 'You were she who abode/ By those red-veined rocks far West'. Emma's distancing to the disputed reality of Cornwall questions the possibility of there ever having been any link between Hardy and this remote being. It asks if they were ever 'we', and only the disintegration of 'I' testifies to the existence of a 'we':

> O you could not know
> That such swift fleeing
> No soul foreseeing –
> Not even I – would undo me so!

In other poems Hardy gives Emma a voice and extends to her an empathy which only her death and the reading of her papers has made possible. The poems mimic the difficulties of all communication, continually recalling the supposed inattention of the hearer, and seeking awkwardly to understand the expectations of the other. 'The Haunter' imagines a tentative, wifely voice for Emma, as she, as a ghost, reiterates her difficulties in attracting attention in life. It is immediately followed by 'The Voice', in which the haunter's plaint is first answered by Hardy, but the achieved communication then dissolves into uncertainty. 'After a Journey', tracking Emma's written recollections through her remembered home landscapes, almost succeeds in giving voice to a 'voiceless ghost'. 'The Phantom

Horsewoman', originally placed as the last poem in the series, grants both the intensity of the haunting and its status as subjective fantasy.[15]

'My spirit will not haunt the mound', a poem of 1913 which appeared elsewhere in *Satires of Circumstance*, also gives Emma a voice, less insistent on attracting attention than 'The Haunter', and humorously resigned to the one-sided nature of all conversation.

> My spirit will not haunt the mound
>   Above my breast,
> But travel, memory possessed,
> To where my tremulous being found
>   Life largest, best.
>
> My phantom-footed shape will go
>   When nightfall grays
> Hither and thither along the ways
> I and another used to know
>   In backward days.
>
> And there you'll find me, if a jot
>   You still should care
> For me and for my curious air;
> If otherwise, then I shall not,
>   For you, be there.

Here Emma, tremulous as in 'The Haunting', engaged in the everyday routines of haunting, reaches in the last stanza toward an exact placing of the relationship between haunter and haunted, speaker and hearer. Like the poems of *Poems of 1912–1913*, it engages in the awkwardness of colloquial intimacy in order to explore an intense experience. It also provides a model for Hardy's own relationship with the reader, one which is conversational, insistently uninsistent, and incorporates an expectation of the reader's inattentiveness. Hardy's reiteration of the merely impressionistic nature of his work includes a pointed unwillingness to insist that the reader's attention should be engaged.

The attention of reviewers in 1914 was not much engaged by *Poems of 1912–1913*, and the later reputation of the series, and particularly of 'After a Journey', 'The Voice' and 'At Castle Boterel', as the summit of Hardy's poetic achievement was not hinted at the time. This was only a final example of the difficulty reviewers in this period encountered in placing Hardy's poetry, a difficulty which Hardy's prefaces were clearly intended to aggravate.

Hardy's various experiments in poetry included the long, three-part, verse drama, The Dynasts, 1904–8, subtitled 'An Epic-Drama of the War with Napoleon', but intended for performance only in the mind's eye. The Dynasts links private lives to public events, but overturns any expectation that the public memory may be more reliable than the private. The historical figures of the Napoleonic Wars are of as questionable reality as Emma's phantom. In a note on the scene of the famous ball given by the Duchess of Richmond on the eve of the Battle of Waterloo, Hardy commented on the difficulty of locating this famous event; 'the spot is almost as phantasmal in its elusive mystery as towered Camelot, the palace of Priam, or the hill of Calvary.'[16] Mythologised in the private memories which accumulate to form the public memory, the status in reality of the Brussels ballroom becomes as uncertain as that of the landscapes of Cornwall in Hardy's memory.

Hardy's anomalous reputation as poet was publicised in December 1908, when his 'A Sunday Morning Tragedy', a poem in traditional ballad form, led off the first number of The English Review. Ford later claimed that it was the news that several other journals had already refused Hardy's poem which secured financial backing for the new journal at a crucial moment. The poem is subtitled 'Circa 186–', but it appropriately prefaced a new journal intending to distinguish itself by its avant-garde attitudes. The subject, a countrywoman's lament for her part in her daughter's fatal backstreet abortion, might be rural, but it was not part of the acceptable rural Hardy.[17]

This Hardy, the exponent of timeless folk values, had an obvious place in a period increasingly obsessed with defining the real England as rural, (see Chapter 3). Quiller-Couch recommended Hardy to his Cambridge students as a genuine aboriginal of the soil.

> First of all, and last of all, he is a countryman. And the first meaning of this is that his mind works like most country minds in this great little

island. They are introspective *because* insular, and their soil is cumbered, piled with history and local tradition.[18]

The terms are very similar to those later evoked by F. R. Leavis in his influential *New Bearings in English Poetry*; 'Hardy was a country-man, and his brooding mind stayed itself habitually upon the simple pieties, the quiet rhythms, and the immemorial ritual of rustic life.'[19] Such attempts to settle Hardy once and for all as an important but archaic figure, firmly placed as countryman, were countered at every stage of his career by his determination not to be so placed. (This resistance itself could be, and was, read as immemorial peasant cussedness.)

The two poems which represented the Edwardian Hardy in the *Oxford Book of Modern Verse*, first published in 1935, were the Trafalgar ballad from *The Dynasts* and the 'Former Beauties' section of 'Casterbridge Fair', choices which demonstrated the view of the editor, Yeats, that Hardy was essentially a balladeer. In his intro-duction he wrote that 'Thomas Hardy, though his work lacked technical accomplishment, made the necessary correction through his mastery of the impersonal objective scene.'[20]

The comment on lack of technique is a central theme in Hardy criticism, often advanced and often refuted, but both parts of the comment bear on Yeats's problems in placing the ballad in its relation to modern poetry. His comment on Hardy is part of a discussion of the facile temptations which the folk tradition offered to modern poets at the turn of the century. Yeats's recognition of the ballad as an important ancestor of modern poetry was tempered by fears of its possible regressive influence.

YEATS: THE STRUGGLE FOR OBJECTIVITY

In his comments on Hardy in 1935 Yeats reiterated his own poetic crisis of the Edwardian period, a time of transition when he repudiated his own past as a poet in the tradition of the Victorian reinterpretation of folk poetry, and insisted on his need to master 'the impersonal objective scene'. His most famous account of this struggle is in a letter to the poet George Russell:

In my *Land of Heart's Desire* and in some of my lyric verse of that time, there is an exaggeration of sentiment and sentimental beauty which I have come to think unmanly. . . . I have been fighting the prevailing decadence for years, and have just got it under foot in my own heart – it is sentiment and sentimental sadness, a womanish introspection. My own early subjectiveness rises at rare moments . . . to a union with a pure energy of the spirit, but between this energy of the spirit and the energy of the will out of which epic and dramatic poetry comes there is a region of brooding emotions full of fleshly waters and vapours which kill the spirit and the will, ecstasy and joy equally. . . . I cannot probably be quite just to any poetry that speaks to me with the sweet insinuating feminine voice of the dwellers in that country of shadows and hollow images. I have dwelt there too long not to dread all that comes out of it.[21]

Yeats was repudiating his own roots in a tradition which he characterised as primitive, regressive and feminine. Yet again the unwanted legacy of Victorianism was typed as feminine, while the emerging modern poetry was 'manly'. Yeats, therefore, had strong personal reasons for being resistant to the poems of Hardy, even if their allegedly regressive amateurish techniques were balanced by a masculine objectivity.

Yeats published three volumes of poems in this period, *In the Seven Woods*, 1904, *The Green Helmet and other Poems*, 1910, and *Responsibilities*, 1914, but included no poems from these works in the *Oxford Book of Modern Verse*. This was his transition period, when he struggled against the siren voices of Victorianism to emerge as the modern poet. The last poem in *Responsibilities*, 'The Coat', summarised this struggle:

> I made my song a coat
> Covered with embroideries
> Out of old mythologies
> From heel to throat;
> But the fools caught it,
> Wore it in the world's eyes
> As though they'd wrought it.
> Song, let them take it,
> For there's more enterprise
> In walking naked.

In 1940 T. S. Eliot suggested that 'Adam's Curse', written in 1902 and included in *In the Seven Woods*, was the key poem of this transition; 'something is coming through, and, in beginning to speak as a particular man, he is beginning to speak for men.'[22] The subject of 'Adam's Curse', the concealed effort behind achieved excellence, was one dear also to Hardy. Samuel Hynes points out a comparable passage in Hardy's *Life*. 'The reviewer so often supposes that where Art is not visible it is unknown to the poet under criticism. Why does he not think of the art concealing art?'[23]

Like Hardy, Yeats is exploring the use of the conversational mode in poetry. The poem describes a talk between two professionals, who are in very different fields but are united by their excellence and their awareness of the cost of that excellence:

> We sat together at one summer's end,
> That beautiful mild woman, your close friend,
> And you and I, and talked of poetry.
> I said 'A line will take us hours maybe;
> Yet if it does not seem a moment's thought,
> Our stitching and unstitching has been naught.'

The apparent effortlessness of the man's writing is matched by the woman's agreement that 'we must labour to be beautiful'; in this debate the woman is granted a professionalism of her own, that of being beautiful. The scene was part of Yeats's ongoing argument with the recalcitrantly political Maud Gonne, to whom the poem is addressed, and the occasion was a remark made by her sister Kathleen that 'It's hard work being beautiful.'[24] In urging Maud to abandon politics for the life of composed beauty which is her true profession, Yeats enlisted her sister in the argument. The easy mellow conversation he recorded conceals the bitterness of the arguments at stake.

Yeats was studying Ben Jonson at this period as a model of professionalism and lyric colloquialism. In this again he resembled Hardy, though, if Hardy's admitted model was 'Drink to me only', Yeats's was 'To Penshurst' and 'The Celebration of Charis', and it was Jonson the poet of public life whom he aspired to follow.

> I am deep in Ben Jonson. . . . I am thinking of writing something on Ben Jonson, or more likely perhaps upon the ideal of life that flitted before the imagination of Jonson or the others when they thought of the Court.[25]

Jonson the Court poet became his ideal of the poet who addressed his audience with ease and assurance. Yeats agreed with Ford that the Victorians had lost the audience for poetry.

In this period Yeats was seeking to redefine himself as a poet speaking to an audience. Several of his major poems are constructed round rhetorical questions and imply a shared community; they include 'No Second Troy', 'Upon a House Shaken by the Land Agitation', and 'September 1913'. In his work for the theatre he was seeking to define a traditional Irish community who would recognise themselves as his audience; his plays in this period included *On Baile's Strand*, 1903, *The King's Threshold*, 1904, *Deirdre*, 1907, and *The Green Helmet*, 1910. In these verse dramas Yeats was attempting to give poetry back a lost inheritance of public importance, though in an entirely different national context from those who advocated English poetry as the repository of the national spirit.

In 1914 Pound, in an enthusiastic review of *Responsibilities* in the new journal *Poetry*, admitted that Yeats's place in modern poetry was uncertain. 'Whenever I mention Mr Yeats I am apt to be assailed with questions. "Will Mr Yeats do anything more?" "Is Yeats in the movement?" "How *can* the chap go on writing this sort of thing?" '[26] To younger poets Yeats was as much a problem as Hardy, a Victorian who refused to accept his place in the past but who could not be placed among the contemporary schools. Pound suggested that Yeats's place in history as a symbolist and balladeer of the late Victorian period was already assured, but he also responded to a new manner he saw Yeats developing, which was characterised by a 'prose directness' as in 'No Second Troy'.

Pound praised the 'greater hardness of outline' in the poems, and the word 'hard' was constantly repeated as the review described the move to objectivity in Yeats's later verse. Pound saw a 'quality of hard light' in 'The Magi', a poem which exemplified Yeats's escape from the siren voices of subjectivity to concentrate on the images themselves:

> Now as at all times I can see in my mind's eye,
> In their stiff painted clothes, the pale unsatisfied ones
> Appear and disappear in the blue depth of the sky
> With all their ancient faces like rain-beaten stones,

And all their helms of silver hovering side by side,
And all their eyes still fixed, hoping to find once more,
Being by Calvary's turbulence unsatisfied,
The uncontrollable mystery on the bestial floor.

By 1914 Yeats had completed his move from his 'unmanly' Victorian past, and remade himself as a poet of hard objectivity. The problem of the identity of the audience for poetry remained. Yeats in his Edwardian poems and poetic dramas was writing for an imagined traditional Irish community; Pound's review suggested that young readers of poetry were baffled by their inability to place Yeats in a modern 'school'. Caught between these two definitions of audience, the popular and the coterie, Yeats in 1914 wrote 'The Fisherman', in which he imagined his ideal audience, a 'sun-freckled' Connemara fisherman, and resolved to write his poetry for this 'man who does not exist,/ A man who is but a dream'.

KIPLING AND LARGE AUDIENCES

The solution of writing to an ideal audience was also suggested by T. S. Eliot in a 1919 review of Kipling's poems.

> It is wrong, of course, of Mr Kipling to address a large audience; but it is a better thing than to address a small one. The only better thing is to address the one hypothetical Intelligent Man who does not exist and who is the audience of the Artist.[27]

Eliot's Intelligent Man is a more abstract concept than Yeats's localised ideal audience, but both felt that by choosing deliberately to write either for a large or for a small audience, the poet was forced to compromise unacceptably.

Kipling, as Eliot suggested, was the contemporary poet most widely known. His great days as a lyricist of empire preceded the twentieth century, but the Edwardian period saw more poems which recorded the responses of Tommy Atkins to the developing imperial situation, for instance 'Chant Pagan', from *The Five Nations*, 1903, in which a Boer War soldier rejects the securities and hierarchies of old England for the freedom of the colonies:

'Ow can I ever take on
With awful old England again,
An' 'ouses both sides of the street,
And 'edges two sides of the lane,
And the parson an' 'gentry' between,
An' touchin' my 'at when we meet –
    Me that 'ave been what I've been?

Much of Kipling's verse of this period, however, celebrated the rural life of 'awful old England', or was historical verse of non-imperialist content, like the two ballads Yeats selected for the *Oxford Book of Modern Verse*, 'Lullaby of St Helena' and 'The Looking-glass'. In his introduction Yeats placed Kipling with Hardy as a balladeer, part of the undeniable but problematic history of poetry. Kipling, however, was described as an urban or 'street' balladeer, rather than rural and 'folk', and thus inferior to Hardy.

Kipling's largest audience, in terms of wide quote-availability, was for two poems which, appropriately in this period, offered definitions of the masculine and feminine respectively. 'If', in its original context in his children's book, *Rewards and Fairies*, 1910, described George Washington, but provided a definition of manliness for politicians on this side of the Atlantic as well. 'The Female of the Species', 1911, was a heavy-duty vehicle for fears of the politicised female, and argued against the granting of suffrage to women in the name of 'that God of abstract justice whom no woman understands'. Both poems are still in public use.

IMAGISM AND IMPRESSIONISM

At the opposite pole to the large audience who found uses for the definitions of manliness in 'If', was the small audience of dedicated poetry readers who asked Pound 'Is Yeats in the movement?' The movement for Pound in 1914 was Imagism. The history and influence of Imagism belong outside a study of the Edwardian period, but between 1908 and 1914 the group of writers associated with Imagism developed the ideal of a hard, objective verse essentially different from the diffuse sentimentalities attributed to

Victorian poetry. While praising Yeats for a similar development, and for imagist passages as in 'The Magi', Pound distinguished Imagism from the symbolism in which Yeats mostly worked. While symbolism moves away from the material to the spiritual, Imagism perceives the image as sufficient in itself. A major influence on the group of poets around Pound who in 1914 produced the anthology, *Des Imagistes*, were the writings of T. E. Hulme, whose most famous essay, 'Romanticism and Classicism', 1912, called for a return from the 'spilt religion' of Romanticism to 'dry and hard' Classicism with its emphasis on 'accurate, precise and definite description'.[28]

Pound was also careful to distinguish Imagism from Impressionism, the mode which his other mentor, Ford, described as the definitive movement in verse and prose at this period.[29] Ford's Impressionism, as defined in his essays 'Impressionism – some Speculations', 1911, and 'On Impressionism', 1914, emphasised the perceiving subject rather than the object perceived. However, in praising Hardy and Yeats as poets who escaped the blight of Victorian diffuseness by concentrating their experience in images, Ford shifted towards Imagism. His ideal audience, also, was Yeatsian; he rejected readers of the *Times Literary Supplement* in favour of a 'granite rock, a peasant intelligence, the gnarled bole of a sempiternal oak'.[30] Impressionism here shifted from its subjective emphasis as Ford's rejection of the Victorians led him, like Yeats and Pound, to extol the objective.

GEORGIAN POETS, THOMAS, MEW

Imagism and Impressionism were international in aspect. The principal home-grown school of the last years before the war was that of the Georgian Poets. The anthology, *Georgian Poetry 1911–1912*, was published in 1912 'in the belief that English poetry is now once again putting on a new strength and beauty' as the editor, Edward Marsh, said in his introductory note.[31] In 1913 Harold Monro established the Poetry Bookshop to promote the importance of poetry, and the four subsequent series of Georgian poetry were produced from there. The Georgians, as their name suggested, were anxious to assert a new identity for themselves, but the Edwardian celebration of Englishness and manliness was still much in evidence. The poem which attracted most attention was Rupert Brooke's 'The Old Vicarage, Grantchester', an exile's lament, written in a Berlin café and partly tongue in cheek, for the synthetic charms of an ostentatiously improbable rural England.

The other much anthologised poem was Walter de la Mare's 'The Listeners', which, like de la Mare's other four poems in the volume, dealt with states of perception out of the normal; this however was not characteristic of the volume. Edward Thomas, reviewing the collection, saw the dominant emphasis as its revelation of 'the modern love of the simple and primitive'. As one example he cited the poem, 'The Fish', where 'Mr Rupert Brooke sincerely . . . and powerfully endeavours to sympathise with a fish and its "dark ecstasies" '.[32] Elsewhere D. H. Lawrence in 'Snapdragon' embraced the possibilities of passionate experience, however dangerous, intimated by that flower.

Several poems were variations on the theme of 'Chant Pagan'. John Masefield, who earlier had written two of the most anthologised Edwardian poems 'Sea Fever', 1902, and 'Cargoes', 1910, remembered the 'bright days' of action, in 'Biography', from the exile of a city of 'miles of shopping women served by men'. W. H. Davies celebrated an ancient mariner, and Wilfred Gibson a poacher. James Elroy Flecker, British vice-consul in Beirut and author of another frontrunning anthology poem, 'The Golden Journey to Samarkand', 1912, contributed two lesser pieces of Orientalising.

Thomas himself did not appear in the anthology; he wrote all his poetry of rural England after the outbreak of World War I, remaking it from the prose works on country travels he had produced for the burgeoning heritage culture of Edwardian England. His poems, apparently produced under the pressure of the war, therefore strictly belong outside the period of this volume. Thomas, like other Edwardians, rejected his immediate ancestors. His discussions with the American poet, Robert Frost, in 1913–14 helped him to evolve a poetry that made use of the rhythms of colloquial speech. His attentiveness to the detail of the countryside he celebrated distinguished that celebration from the easy pastoralism which provided a market for his prose works. In describing his kind of patriotism in the poem 'This is no case of petty right or wrong', 1915, he sought to distinguish his England from the England of the imperialists, and in 'Lob', 1915, he constructed an English rural mythology more radical in emphasis than the mythologies of *Howards End* or *Puck of Pook's Hill*.

In the Edwardian literary scene, in which the emphasis was on escape from Victorian sentimentalism into a new, manly, objective poetry, the role available for women poets must have been difficult to discern. Charlotte Mew, that distinctly unheeded siren voice, seems to be the appropriate representative. Hardy described her as 'the greatest poetess I have come across lately, in my judgment, though so meagre in her output',[33] and Woolf found her 'very good and interesting and unlike anyone else'.[34]

Mew was writing poetry throughout the Edwardian period, and Monro, without success, urged her poem 'The Farmer's Bride' on Marsh as the first, token, woman's poem for the third Georgian anthology of 1916. The rejected 'The Farmer's Bride', like her other most famous poem, 'The Changeling', treats of an alienated being whose life is outside the comprehension of the normal. The speaker is male, a farmer whose work routine is interrupted by his feral bride, and who realises through her alienation from him his own division from nature:

> The short days shorten and the oaks are brown,
>   The blue smoke rises to the low grey sky,
> One leaf in the still air falls slowly down,
>   A magpie's spotted feathers lie
> On the black earth spread white with rime,
> The berries redden up to Christmas time.
>   What's Christmas time without there be
>   Some other in the house than we!
>
>   She sleeps up in the attic there
>   Alone, poor maid. 'Tis but a stair
> Betwixt us. Oh! my God! the down,
> The soft young down of her, the brown,
> The brown of her – her eyes, her hair, her hair![35]

Mew's choice of a male speaker to articulate the situation of his bride, whom he finds beyond human comprehension, suggests a very considerable alienation from the art in which she was working.

Chapter 7

The New Novel

In 1914 Henry James published an article, 'The younger generation', in the *Times Literary Supplement* which assessed the contemporary state of the novel. Later that year he expanded and republished it in *Notes on Novelists* under the title 'The New Novel'. The article made reference to a dozen novelists, including established writers such as Bennett and Wells, and newcomers such as Lawrence. As a piece of talent spotting the article was not a great success; James thought that Lawrence should 'hang in the dusty rear',[1] and backed Hugh Walpole and Compton Mackenzie as the coming novelists. The significance of 'The New Novel' lay in James's contention that the tendency of contemporary fiction was regressive. This accusation was influential in establishing the idea that the English novel was in crisis.

To James no narrative point of view was artistically possible except that of the consciousness of the individual character. He rejected the claim to objective authority of the authorial commentator, and the confessional formlessness of the first person narrator. His reviews of his Victorian predecessors consistently criticised their lack of that sense of composition in the novel which French writers such as Flaubert exemplified. To the senior novelist in English at the end of his career the work of his younger contemporaries seemed an exaggeration of this Victorian deficiency, its main characteristic a 'saturation' with circumstantial evidence.

James took Bennett, and specifically *Clayhanger* and *Hilda*

Lessways, as his examples of Edwardian 'saturation'. He described these novels as vast accumulations:

> a monument exactly not to an idea, a pursued and captured meaning, or in short *to* anything whatever, but just simply *of* the quarried and gathered material it happens to contain, the stones and bricks and rubble and cement and promiscuous constituents of every sort that have been heaped in it and thanks to which it quite massively piles itself up. Our perusal and our enjoyment are our watching of the growth of the pile and of the capacity, industry, energy, with which the operation is directed. (pp. 369–70)

Bennett criticised the Victorians' deficiencies of form as vigorously as James did, insisting for his part on his debt to the French naturalists with their exact documentation of material and economic environment. James had already used the building metaphor in a 1903 article on the major practitioner of naturalism, Zola. 'The pyramid had been planned and the site staked out, but the young builder stood there, in his sturdy strength, with no equipment save his two hands and, as we may say, his wheel-barrow and his trowel.'[2] Zola, like his admirer, Bennett, is described as a builder in a very humble line. James's admiration for the materialist emphasis of naturalism was very limited, but he admitted that naturalism and Zola at least had a plan. Bennett's heaps of variegated material remained simply accumulation.

JAMES: *THE WINGS OF THE DOVE*

When James described his own methods, as in the preface to *The Wings of the Dove*, building became architecture. He spoke of 'sufficiently solid *blocks* of wrought material, squared to the sharp edge, as to have weight and mass and carrying power; to make for construction, that is, to produce for effect and to provide for beauty.'[3] James's 'compositional key' was his adoption of the point of view of individual characters as the basic narrative method. The preface insisted that there was no 'superior process' to that by which the narrative of *The Wings of the Dove* moves through successive centres of consciousness. James's three great novels of the Edwardian period, *The Wings of the Dove*, 1902, *The Ambassadors*, 1903, first written but second published, and *The Golden Bowl*, 1904, are his final demonstration of this method of working a heap into a monument.

The description of Bennett suggested analogies not only with building, but with finance. Bennett accumulated his material, but could not work it profitably. The analogy of art with high finance is suggested throughout *The Wings of the Dove*, appropriately, for this novel set in the world of plutocracy. The terrifying power of those in whose hands vast wealth is concentrated was a major topic of this period. Works which attempted to understand the opportunities and motives of these extraordinary beings included Conrad's *Nostromo*, Wells's *Tono-Bungay*, and Shaw's *Major Barbara*, as well as the *Dove* and *The Golden Bowl*. James's protagonist is not a great financier, but a terminally ill young woman, Milly Theale, an American 'heiress of all the ages',[4] on whom the accumulated fortunes of a great American financial family have descended. Courted for her wealth by the male partner of two lovers who have discovered her mortal sickness, she dies aware of his treachery but still willing him her fortune.

The theme of the criminal associations of great money dominates James's novels of this period. The novel, *The Ivory Tower*, unfinished at his death, hovers around the deathbed of a man 'just dying of twenty millions' and of 'the things you do for it', and the problems of his heiress, taking up the burden of great resources, 'dishonoured and stained and blackened at their very roots'.[5] He was still working over the material of *The Wings of the Dove*. Milly inherits the concentrated wealth of her civilisation, and is thus potentially criminal; her hands 'imbrued' (p. 293), as the preface puts it, with the generosity and extravagance her great wealth allows. It is this generosity which provokes the squalid conspiracy, but in her final act she transcends her wealth and justifies the civilisation she inherited; 'she stretched out her wings and it was to that they reached' (Ch. 38).

In the preface to *The Wings of the Dove* James persistently used financial analogies to describe his operations as author, He said of his subject that 'it might have a great deal to give, but would probably ask for equal services in return, and would collect this debt to the last shilling' (p. 289), and he described the effects of his heroine's situation as analogous to those produced by 'the failure of a great business' (p. 293). The repetition of such references emphasises the relation between his situation and Milly's. James, like his heroine, was an operator in high finance, a heavily endowed figure seeking to extract the utmost value possible from his sordid accumulation of wealth.

James described his subject in the preface as 'one of those chances for good taste, possibly even for the play of the very best in the world' (p. 289). The opportunity came precisely from the squalor of the subject, which would emphasise by contrast the art produced from it. The entries in his *Notebooks* reveal how deeply James was concerned that this subject should not remain 'vulgarly ugly'.[6] The base materials were to be transformed into aesthetic form by his narrative method, and by the increasing abstraction of his style in this period, the intangibility documented in detail in the work of Ian Watt and of Seymour Chatman.[7]

James's preoccupation with the lives of the very rich appeared bafflingly dilettante to many. Masterman, in *The Condition of England*, commented representatively on 'the extraordinary analysis by Mr Henry James of the meaning of situation in various companies of rich, idle persons whose utility or significance in any rational universe it is difficult to apprehend.'[8] It was, however, the sheer density of material circumstance James indicated that provided the conditions from which he and his protagonists produced value. He is continuously aware of the dependence of the worlds of artistic or moral value upon the material world, and of the increasing power and grossness of the financial interest. In the last paragraph of the preface to *The Wings of the Dove* he described Milly as appearing to the reader as an 'unspotted princess', a 'mystic figure in the gilded coach', observed by the vulgar from balconies and other vantage points. In that age of the 'invention of tradition', the role of art, like that of royalty, was to present a symbolic value which justified, and momentarily effaced, the material civilisation on which it was based.

THE JAMES-WELLS DISPUTE

'The New Novel' brought to a head James's long-standing argument with Wells about the role of fiction. Wells saw the older novelist as the main representative of an aesthetic which increasingly isolated fiction from the contemporary world. James reserved his harshest language in the article for Wells. If Bennett's work resembled mere barbaric accumulation, Wells's figured as excreted waste:

> The more this author learns and learns, or at any rate knows and knows, however, the greater is this impression of his holding it good enough for us, such as we are, that he shall but turn out his mind and its contents upon us by any free familiar gesture and as from a high window forever open. (p. 371)

The grossness of the image expressing James's distaste for the material circumstance in which he saw Wells's work immersed, was the public culmination of a series of private comments (in letters) by James to Wells throughout the period.

Love and Mr Lewisham in 1900 was 'a bloody little chunk of life'. *Kipps* in 1905 was 'raw' in its awareness of 'the shockingly sick actuality of things'. In 1906 James complained of *In the Days of the Comet* that

> one doesn't, in it, take refuge, (one can't), in the waiting-room of the Crematorium, with a saddened sense of the great Process going on *adjacently* – one is in presence of the heated oven and one hears and feels the roar and scorch of the flames.

Of *Ann Veronica*, 1909, he said that 'the total result lives and kicks and throbs and flushes and glares.'

Writing of *The New Machiavelli*, 1911, James admonished Wells for 'your big feeling for life, your capacity for chewing up the thickness of the world in such enormous mouthfuls, while you fairly slobber, so to speak, with the multitudinous taste'.[9] James progresses logically and coherently from the 'rawness' of *Love and Mr Lewisham* and *Kipps* to the gross chewing of *The New Machiavelli*, and thence to the waste product described in 'The New Novel'. The violence of these images, half-concealed within the exquisite periphrases of his late manner, indicated his total rejection of a mode of writing which he saw as wholly unselective.

In the earlier part of the period James had had hopes of Wells, whose interest in Utopias he saw as encouraging evidence of a kindred wish for an art which kept a sophisticated distance from the rawness of actuality. In 1902 he was sufficiently sympathetic to *The First Men in the Moon* to wish to rewrite it in his own terms, a suggestion which now seems to us bizarre. At the time of the publication of *Kipps* he was still able to describe Wells as 'the most interesting "literary man" of your generation – in fact the only interesting one.' As the decade wore on, however, he tended increasingly to see Wells as someone who had 'cut loose from literature clearly – practically altogether'. In this he followed Kipling, an earlier James protégé, until his fascination with modern technology distracted him from producing anything James could describe as literature.[10]

The story of the disagreement is complicated by Wells's readiness to accept the positions James outlined for him. He adopted the violence of James's language in talking about his work, agreeing, for instance, that *The New Machiavelli* should be 'the last of my gushing Hari-Karis [sic]'.[11] In more general terms he accepted James's view that his writing was not 'literature', and in so doing accepted the dichotomy which James believed existed between mandarin literature and rough-and-ready journalism, a dichotomy which was to have considerable consequences for the history of the novel.

Wells's lack of interest in form was epitomised for James by his frequent use of the first person narrator. In his preface to *The Ambassadors*, James outlined his compositional law for that novel 'of employing but one centre and keeping it all within my hero's compass'. *The Wings of the Dove* used several centres of consciousness. *The Ambassadors* employed only one, but James's construction of his narrative within the limited perception of his New England widower, Lambert Strether, achieved quite different effects from those achievable through the use of a first person narrator. That method James described in his preface as the 'terrible *fluidity* of self-revelation'[12]. Writing to Wells about *The New Machiavelli*, he talks of 'the bad service you have done your cause by riding so hard again that accurst autobiographic form which puts a premium on the loose, the improvised, the cheap and the easy.'[13]

Wells's previous use of the first person was in his most adventurous novel, *Tono-Bungay*, on which James found himself too 'stultified' to comment.[14] The narrator, George, points out at the beginning that the realist modes of the nineteenth century are no longer appropriate to the twentieth-century experiences to be discussed. His comments also suggest why Wells's ideas about the novel were so opposed to James's:

> I realise what a fermenting mass of things learnt and emotions experienced and theories formed I've got to deal with, and how, in a sense, hopeless my book must be from the very outset. I suppose what I'm really trying to render is nothing more nor less than Life – as one man has found it. . . . do what I will I fail to see I can be other than a lax, undisciplined story-teller. I must sprawl and flounder, comment and theorise, if I am to get out the thing I have in mind. And it isn't a constructed tale I have to tell but unmanageable realities. Part I, Ch. 1

In his *Experiment in Autobiography* Wells described the early twentieth century as a time of crisis for fiction. The nineteenth-century model, 'the play of individuals in a rigid scheme of values never more to be questioned or permanently changed', ceased to be available to the serious novelist:

> The novel in England was produced in an atmosphere of security for the entertainment of secure people who liked to feel established and safe for good. Its standards were fixed within that apparently permanent frame and the criticism of it began to be irritated and perplexed when, through a new instability, the splintering frame began to get into the picture.[15]

In *Tono-Bungay* the relation of the frame to the picture is problematical throughout. On the first page George tells us that his experiences of rapid upward mobility make it impossible for him to structure his life within existing fictional forms. The English novel, he suggests, developed to describe a firmly fixed social hierarchy, where people played very clearly defined roles as if they were character actors. His experience has been different, and there is no existing fictional mode for describing his journey from the servant class to plutocracy, and then to bankruptcy and eventual exile. 'One gets hit by some unusual transverse force, one is jerked out of one's stratum and lives crosswise for the rest of time, and, as it were, in a succession of samples.' George's deracination is presented as a characteristic early twentieth-century experience, for which earlier fiction forms were inappropriate, evolved as they were to describe a world where class mobility and cultural and moral relativism were rare.

This belief that the fixed Victorian society had suddenly disintegrated, and that radical changes were required in the literary forms which had described it, was dominant in the period. Edwardian writers perceived themselves as in a phase of dynamic upheaval after long stasis, although this perception can be found among writers of the later Victorian period also. In 1914 Lawrence was complaining about those past writers who attempted 'to conceive a character in a certain moral scheme and make him consistent', and saying 'you mustn't look in my novel for the old stable *ego* of the character.'[16] Like Wells he was concerned with the splintering frame and its relation to the picture.

In *Tono-Bungay* the disintegrating relations between literature and society which the novel describes are explained by a particular historical view, the dominant myth of the country house which froze all attempts at the dynamic restructuring English society so desperately needed (see Chapter 3). In the same way, Wells suggested, the literary forms which evolved to celebrate that myth continued to exert their freezing grip on fiction's popular interpretation of society's needs. Just as *Tono-Bungay* describes George's attempts to escape Bladesover House, so Wells was attempting to escape the traditional novel, and disintegrate the fixed relation of frame and picture in the novel. In the younger novelist's interpretation of the literary crisis, James was not an artistic innovator, but a writer who accepted the social hierarchies of Bladesover.

Wells responded to James's criticisms in 'The New Novel' in his satire *Boon*, 1915. *Boon* purported to be the posthumously published work of an eminent writer, which he had kept secret from his repressively respectable female secretary. One chapter attacked James through a discussion of his work followed by a parody synopsis of a novel in his manner. The attack brought the long-standing argument to an end. James's response was elegant and conclusive. 'It is difficult of course for a writer to put himself *fully* in the place of another writer who finds him extraordinarily futile and void, and who is moved to publish that to the world.' Wells's reply characteristically adopted a Jamesian view of his work. He suggested that *Boon* was to be seen merely as a waste-paper basket, to which James retorted unarguably that the contents of such receptacles were what one precisely did not publish.

Wells's main justification for attacking James was that he was 'altogether too dominant in the world of criticism'. In *Boon* James represented not artistic experiment but a stifling of response to the rapidly evolving conditions of life.

> He doesn't find things out. He doesn't even seem to want to find things out. You can see that in him; he is eager to accept things – elaborately. You can see from his books that he accepts etiquettes, precedences, associations, claims. That is his peculiarity. He accepts very readily and then – elaborates. He has, I am convinced, one of the strongest, most abundant minds alive in the whole world, and he has the smallest penetration. Indeed, he has no penetration.[17]

Wells's view of James here can be related to a 1902 article, 'The discovery of the future', in *Nature*, where he defined two kinds of mind. The majority mind, which he called the 'legal or submissive', is ruled by precedent and the established order of things, while the creative mind can envisage change; on the latter the future of humanity depends. James, as described in *Boon*, clearly belonged to the former category. Wells argued in 'The discovery of the future' that 'literature is for the most part history, or history at one remove', and it was this literary bias to the historical, so eminently represented by James, that Wells wanted to change. Literature had an inadequate sense of its responsibilities at 'the beginning of the greatest change that humanity has ever undergone'.[18]

Wells's readiness to accept James's exclusion of him from 'literature' sprang partly from his own categorising of 'literature' as a particular kind of conservative, precedent-ridden writing. The novel was something different and had an important part to play in the new writing which would create the future. In his major discussion of the role of fiction, the 1911 lecture, 'The Contemporary Novel', Wells argued that the novel was 'the only medium through which we can discuss the great majority of the problems which are being raised in such bristling multitude by our contemporary social development.'[19]

Wells saw James as opposed to this kind of discussion in fiction; he claimed in *Boon* that 'James's selection becomes just omission and nothing more. He omits everything that demands digressive treatment or collateral statement. For example, he omits opinions.'[20] In urging the case in his lecture for a more socially conscious novel Wells found himself turning back to the derided Victorians, and thus cutting himself off from the more innovative trends in modern fiction.

Each writer saw the other as an traditionalist opposing experiment. James saw Wells as a journalist treating social questions, falling back on the ramshackle, outmoded methods of the age of Dickens. To Wells, James was a precedent-bound mandarin, perpetuating his views through an institution called 'Literature'. When James urged Wells in 1912 to join the newly formed Academic Committee to promote the dignity of literature, Wells replied 'I have an insurmountable objection to Literary or Artistic Academies as such, to any hierarchies, any suggestion of controls or fixed standards in these things.'[21]

Their mutual misunderstanding established an opposition between formal experiment and social concern in the novel which was significant for later developments in the novel. In their own fiction the opposition was not so fixed; *Tono-Bungay* was formally innovative, and *The Wings of the Dove* acute about social relations in the plutocratic society of Edwardian England. In their disagreement, however, they agreed on the existence of division in fictional practices. Innovative fiction, in James's wake, became associated with the private and psychological, while the discussion of social problems which Wells had urged as the novel's crucial role was left to the 'documentary' methods of more traditional fiction, or to the genre of science fiction he had pioneered. Raymond Williams in *The English Novel from Dickens to Lawrence* suggests in the chapter on James and Wells, 'A parting of the ways', that the choice they forced upon their successors was an indication of the increasing unadaptability and exclusiveness of English culture.[22]

CONRAD AND THE MULTIPLIED PRODUCER

The apparent hero of contemporary fiction in 'The New Novel' was Conrad, whom James cited as 'absolutely alone as a votary of the way to do a thing that shall make it undergo most doing' (p. 379). By this he meant that Conrad was the only writer among the younger generation to have understood the importance of the point of view in narrative method. The novel discussed was *Chance* with which Conrad in 1914 achieved his first popular success. In *Chance* the story is presented through successive points of view, as various characters, co-ordinated by Conrad's favourite narrator, Marlow, attempt to understand the central situation.

James commented on Conrad's transference of the reader's interest from this situation to the method by which it was observed and recounted, by

> so multiplying his creators or, as we are now fond of saying, producers, as to make them almost more numerous and quite emphatically more material than the creatures and the production itself in whom and which we by the general law of fiction expect such agents to lose themselves. (pp. 380-1)

Conrad had employed these multiplied producers of point of view in his earlier works of the decade, *Lord Jim*, *Nostromo*, *The Secret Agent*, and *Under Western Eyes*, but in the inferior *Chance* the method reached a degree of complication surpassed only by James's description of it.

James's suggestion that Conrad's interest lay entirely in formal experiment was a misrepresentation. Conrad's 'producers' differ considerably from James's. In James these agents are observers, indeed, as Seymour Chatman has demonstrated in his *The Later Style of Henry James*, mostly passive observers on whose attention observations are forced; 'the human perceiver is regularly object rather than subject.'[23] Conrad's producers are engaged in efforts to reconstruct the traditional story-telling situation, to evoke the 'solidarity' of an audience.

In his major aesthetic statement, the preface to *The Nigger of the Narcissus*, 1897, Conrad attempted to bridge the widening gulf between the subjective artist and his audience. He described how the artist, in 'a single-minded attempt to render the highest kind of justice to the visible universe', appeals successfully to his audience when he 'descends within himself, and . . . finds the terms of his appeal'. What the artist returns with will be only a 'rescued fragment', but it may be enough to 'awaken in the hearts of the beholders that feeling of unavoidable solidarity . . . which binds men to each other and all mankind to the visible world.'[24]

While the preface expressed confidence that the artist's subjective exploration will enable him to communicate with his audience, two articles of 1905 suggested less assurance about the power of art to evoke this solidarity. In his major political essay, 'Autocracy and war', Conrad commented on the failure of newspaper reports to communicate any imaginative realisation of the current Russo–Japanese War. 'Direct vision of the fact, or the stimulus of a great art', he argued, were the only experiences which could awaken the Western imagination, but he added that art ran the danger of arousing 'a purely aesthetic admiration of the rendering'.[25] James's response to *Chance* must have confirmed this fear.

In an article on James in 1905 Conrad evoked, as in the preface to *The Nigger of the Narcissus*, the heroic activity of the writer; 'the creative art of a writer of fiction may be compared to rescue work carried out in darkness against cross gusts of wind swaying the action of a great multitude.' There was, however, a significant shift in his attitude to the potential audience. The preface's hopeful appeal to the 'solidarity' of humanity gave way to a realisation that the artist's heroic innovation may be difficult to reconcile with the uncomplicated desires of his audience. 'Perhaps the only true desire of mankind, coming thus to light in its hours of leisure, is to be set at rest. One is never set at rest by Mr Henry James's novels.'[26]

Both articles offered warnings about the dangers inherent in an art which seeks a 'purely aesthetic admiration'. Conrad's experiments with point of view and disrupted chronology classed him as

foremost among those writers breaking with established lite
forms. Ford, his closest literary friend and occasional collaborator,
described him as the prime exponent of Impressionism, and in his
memoir, *Joseph Conrad: A personal reminiscence*, presented their
commitment to Impressionism as the innovative enterprise of the
period; 'we saw that life did not narrate, but made impressions on
our brains. We in turn, if we wished to produce on you an effect of
life, must not narrate but render . . . impressions.'[27]

Conrad, however, was reluctant to accept the implied loss of
audience as James had done. He wished also to narrate. Fredric
Jameson in *The Political Unconscious* argues that Conrad's fictions
embodied the increasingly marked division between high and mass
culture. Critically accepted as part of the avant-garde of consciously
aesthetic fiction, they still sought to recreate a more traditional and
popular story-telling situation. There was Conrad, the experimental
aesthete, but there was also Conrad the sea dog and teller of yarns.
Indeed when Conrad died in 1924, the latter reputation was
temporarily dominant. Ernest Hemingway obituarised him as
someone despised by the literary élite. 'And now he's dead and I
wish to God they would have taken some great acknowledged
technician of a literary figure and left him to write his bad stories.'[28]

AFTER 1914

In 1915 Conrad's disciple, Ford, published his major novel, *The
Good Soldier*, which summarised his reaction against the English
fictional tradition. He later quoted an admirer who described it as
'the finest French novel in the English language',[29] praise which
confirmed Ford's hope that his novel could be seen as existing in the
European tradition of commitment to formal perfection exemplified
by such writers as Flaubert and Maupassant. In *The Good Soldier* the
American narrator, Dowell, attempts to organise his memories and
impressions of the complicated series of adulterous liaisons in the
vicinity of which he has existed, uncomprehending, for the past
decade. The points of view of the participants form much of his

evidence, and the narrative sequence disrupts chronology to follow his memories.

Although Ford had already written several novels, including two in collaboration with Conrad, this was his major demonstration of Impressionism. Confined within Dowell's limited perceptions, the reader has no access to any authoritative ordering of events. The author is invisible, fulfilling Ford's dictum that 'the Impressionist author is sedulous to avoid letting his personality appear in the course of his book.'[30] It is no longer possible to take for granted a known audience either. Dowell comments explicitly on the difficulties for narration posed by this absence of audience. In the great English country house which has become his property, with no company but a deranged English girl incapable of hearing him, he attempts to imagine an ideal listener. 'So I shall just imagine myself for a fortnight or so at one side of the fireplace of a country cottage, with a sympathetic soul opposite me' (Part I, Ch. 2).

Dowell soon regrets the absence of a recognisable audience to direct his narrative. 'Is all this digression or isn't it digression? Again I don't know. You, the listener, sit opposite me. But you are so silent. You don't tell me anything' (Part I, Ch. 2). In this Conradian regret for the loss of audience, as in its picture of English gentlefolk 'stepping a minuet' (Part I, Ch. 1) on the brink of catastrophe, *The Good Soldier* hankers for the apparent securities of prewar England. The novel is in part an epitaph for the lost illusions of a mythical Edwardian afternoon.

In 1914 two major collections of short stories by two writers who had moved beyond such regrets were published. Lawrence's *The Prussian Officer* reprinted 'Odour of Chrysanthemums' and 'Goose Fair', the two stories which had been his first published work, accepted by Ford for *The English Review*. Ford later recalled that he proclaimed Lawrence as a genius on the strength of reading the first paragraph of 'Odour of Chrysanthemums', which revealed a writer with the exact consciousness of language and composition hitherto lacking in the English tradition.[31] ('Goose Fair', however, was the earlier published of the two.) For Lawrence this tradition was dead, and 'Conrad and such folks – the Writers among the Ruins' failed to realise it.[32]

The same year also saw the long delayed publication of Joyce's first prose work, the series of short stories, *Dubliners*. Its 'style of scrupulous meanness'[33] associated it with the French school of naturalism, but the naturalistic details were raised to symbolic intensity. Pound praised its modern reconciliation of subjective and objective. 'Mr Joyce writes a clear hard prose. He deals with subjective things, but he presents them with such clarity of outline that he might be dealing with locomotives or with builders' specifications.'[34]

Also in 1914 *A Portrait of the Artist as a Young Man* began serialisation in *The Egoist*. Its hero, Stephen Dedalus, moved towards an acceptance that exile was the necessary condition for the artist. Stephen's formula for the artist's presence in his work resembled Ford's for the invisible Impressionist. 'The artist, like the God of creation, remains within or behind or beyond or above his handiwork, invisible, refined out of existence, indifferent, paring his fingernails.'[35]

The accepted image of the prewar generation was established by Woolf's two influential essays, 'Modern Fiction', 1919, and 'Mr Bennett and Mrs Brown', 1924. Woolf created a three-headed monster, Wells–Bennett–Galsworthy to represent the Edwardian novel. She adopted James's criticism of the 'saturation' methods of the Edwardians but her polemical aims were rather different from James's; she needed a representation of the Edwardian patriarchy in whose heyday she had written her first novel with so much difficulty, and whose bankruptcy in the modern world she wished to demonstrate. The Edwardian novelist, 'taking upon his shoulders the work that ought to have been discharged by Government officials', had failed his successors by his use of tools and conventions developed to describe a purely material universe. 'For us those conventions are ruin, those tools are death.'[36]

Woolf's indictment of the Edwardians for their failure to evolve techniques to treat the subjectivity of Mrs Brown moves uncertainly between modernism and feminism. They talked about the 'fabric of things', she suggested, as a hostess talks about the weather, to establish a polite but superficial relation with the guest/reader. It was an analogy she repeated when, in reviewing *A Passage to India*, she praised Forster for escaping the hostessy manner of his Edwardian novels. 'Hitherto Mr Forster has been apt to pervade his novels like a careful hostess who is anxious to introduce, to explain, to warn her guests of a step here, of a draught there.'[37] But if Edwardian novelists were typed as hostessy, as observing the extinct conventions of a lost world, they were also seen as violent patriarchal males, denying Mrs Brown her identity and insisting on their own rights over her being.

In a later attack of the 1920s Woolf's three-headed monster was reproduced by Rebecca West, another of the woman writers who had begun writing in the Edwardian period. In her article, 'Uncle Bennett', she added Shaw to the original trio, and described them as the 'uncles', old-fashioned, domineering males, bringing presents to the public they saw as their children.[38] It was further evidence that the Edwardians, who saw themselves as rebels, were presented to the next generation as oppressive patriarchs. This was perhaps fair comment on Edwardian assertiveness but it partly misrepresented the writers of the period. They had also recognised a breakdown of consensus about what English literature was, and who produced it for whom. They saw themselves as witnessing 'the beginning of the greatest change that humanity has ever undergone'. Their major works attempted to come to terms with such recognitions.

Notes

References to novels are to chapters, not pages, and after the first citation appear in the text.

CHAPTER 1

1. Virginia Woolf, *The Voyage Out* (Grafton, London, 1986), Ch. 24.
2. Florence Hardy, *The Life of Thomas Hardy* (Macmillan, London, 1962), p. 444.
3. John Keats, *The Letters 1814–1821*, ed. Hyder Rollins (Cambridge University Press, Cambridge, 1958), p. 394.
4. Samuel Hynes, *Edwardian Occasions* (Routledge & Kegan Paul, London, 1972), pp. 191–208.
5. See Chris Baldick, *The Social Mission of English Criticism 1848–1932* (Clarendon Press, Oxford, 1983), pp. 59–85; Peter Brooker and Peter Widdowson, 'A literature for England', in *Englishness: Politics and Culture 1880–1920*, ed. Robert Colls and Philip Dodd (Croom Helm, London, 1986), pp. 116–63; Brian Doyle, *English and Englishness* (Routledge, London, 1989); Terry Lovell, *Consuming Fiction* (Verso, London, 1987).
6. David Cannadine, 'The British monarchy c. 1820–1977', in *The Invention of Tradition*, ed. Eric Hobsbawm and Terence Ranger (Cambridge University Press, Cambridge, 1983), pp. 101–64.

7. Ford Madox Ford, 'Impressionism – some speculations', in *Critical Writings of Ford Madox Ford*, ed. Frank MacShane (University of Nebraska Press, Lincoln, 1964), pp. 143–5.

8. Virginia Woolf, *The Captain's Deathbed* (Hogarth Press, London, 1950), p. 91.

9. *Oxford Book of Modern Verse 1892–1935*, ed. W. B. Yeats (Clarendon Press, Oxford, 1936), p. xi.

10. Edward Thomas, *A Language not to be Betrayed: Selected prose*, ed. Edna Langley (Carcanet, Manchester, 1981), p. 113.

11. Arnold Bennett, *Books and Persons* (Chatto & Windus, London, 1917), p. 42.

12. Ford Madox Ford, *Memories and Impressions*, ed. Michael Killigrew (Penguin, Harmondsworth, 1979), p. 200. See also Malcolm Bradbury, 'The English Review', *The London Magazine*, Vol. 5 (1958) pp. 46–57.

13. Louise de Salvo *Virginia Woolf's First Voyage: A novel in the making* (Macmillan, London, 1980).

14. Raymond Williams, *Politics and Letters* (New Left Books, London, 1979), p. 263.

15. N. N. Feltes, *Modes of Production of Victorian Novels* (Chicago University Press, Chicago, 1986), pp. 36–57.

16. Hynes, *Edwardian Occasions*, pp. 196–202.

17. *Henry James and H. G. Wells*, ed. Leon Edel and Gordon Ray (Hart-Davis, London, 1958), p. 160; p. 164.

18. Isaiah Berlin, 'Beloved monster', in the *Guardian*, 12 October 1989, p. 25.

19. Rudyard Kipling, *Kipling's Verse: A definitive edition* (Hodder & Stoughton, London, 1946), p. 332.

20. *Henry James: Selected literary criticism*, ed. Morris Shapira (Penguin, Harmondsworth, 1963), p. 269.

21. G. K. Chesterton, *The Victorian Age in Literature* (Williams & Norgate, London, 1913), pp. 102–3.

22. Bennett, *Books and Persons*, p. 135.

23. *Arnold Bennett: The Evening Standard years*, ed. Andrew Mylett (Chatto & Windus, London, 1974), p. 71.

24. Arnold Bennett, *The Letters*, ed. James Hepburn (Oxford University Press, London, 1968), Vol. II, p. 104.

25. Arthur Quiller-Couch, *On the Art of Writing* (Cambridge University Press, Cambridge, 1919), pp. 247–8.

26. Woolf, *The Captain's Deathbed*, p. 87.

27. Sandra Gilbert and Susan Gubar, *No Man's Land: The place of the woman writer in the twentieth century*, Vol. I, *The War of the*

Words, and Vol. II, *Sexchanges* (Yale University Press, New Haven, 1988–9).

28. Henry James, 'The next time', in *'The Figure in the Carpet' and Other Stories*, ed. Frank Kermode (Penguin, Harmondsworth, 1986), p. 350.

29. Peter Keating, *The Haunted Study: A social history of the English novel 1875–1914*, (Secker & Warburg, London, 1989), pp. 369–445.

30. Bennett, *Books and Persons*, pp. 99–100.

31. H. G. *Wells's Literary Criticism*, ed. Patrick Parrinder and Robert Philmus (Harvester Wheatsheaf, Hemel Hempstead, 1980), p. 74.

32. Edel and Ray, p. 134.

33. Henry James, *The Art of the Novel*, ed. R. P. Blackmur (Scribner, New York, 1962), p. 227.

34. Woolf, *The Captain's Deathbed*, p. 99: Bennett, *Books and Persons*, p. 232.

CHAPTER 2

1. *Wells's Literary Criticism*, p. 98.

2. Joseph Conrad, *Nostromo* (Penguin, Harmondsworth, 1963), Part III, Ch. 1.

3. See Isobel Quigley, *The Heirs of Tom Brown* (Oxford University Press, Oxford, 1984); *Imperialism and Juvenile Literature*, ed. Jeffrey Richards (Manchester University Press, Manchester, 1989).

4. See Christine Bolt, *Victorian Attitudes to Race* (Routledge & Kegan Paul, London, 1971); Patrick Brantlinger, *The Rule of Darkness: British literature and imperialism, 1830–1914* (Cornell University Press, Ithaca, 1988); Joanna de Groot, ' "Sex" and "Race": The construction of language and image in the nineteenth century', in *Sexuality and Subordination: Studies of gender in the nineteenth century*, ed. Susan Mendus and Jane Rendall (Routledge, London, 1989), pp. 89–128; Lewis Wurgaft, *The Imperial Imagination: Magic and myth in Kipling's India* (Wesleyan University Press, Middletown, 1983).

5. See Louis James, 'Tom Brown's imperialist sons', *Victorian Studies*, Vol. 17 (1973) pp. 89–99.

6. George Orwell, *Collected Essays, Journals and Letters*, ed. Sonia Orwell and Ian Angus (Penguin, Harmondsworth, 1971), Vol. I, p. 518.

7. Eric Hobsbawm, *The Age of Empire* (Weidenfeld & Nicholson, London, 1987), p. 70.

8. Andrew Lang, 'Realism and romance', *Contemporary Review*, p. 52 (1887) pp. 683–93.

9. See *Imperialism and Juvenile Literature*; Martin Green, *Dreams of Adventure, Deeds of Empire* (Basic Books, New York, 1979).

10. George Gissing, *The Whirlpool* (Harvester Wheatsheaf, Hemel Hempstead, 1977), Part III, Ch. 13.

11. See G. Searle, *The Quest for National Efficiency* (Blackwell, Oxford, 1971).

12. Kipling, *Kipling's Verse*, p. 300.

13. Joseph Conrad, *Collected Letters*, ed. Frederick Karl and Laurence Davies (Cambridge University Press, Cambridge, 1986), Vol. II, pp. 139–40.

14. Joseph Conrad, *Heart of Darkness* in *Three Short Novels* (Bantam, New York, 1963), Ch. 2.

15. Conrad, *Letters*, Vol. II, p. 210; Vol. II, p. 207.

16. T. H. Huxley, *'Evolution and Ethics' and other essays* (Macmillan, London, 1895), pp. 1–116.

17. John Hobson, *The Psychology of Jingoism* (Grant Richards, London, 1901), p. 40; John Robertson, *Wrecking the Empire* (Grant Richards, London, 1901), p. 228.

18. D. H. Lawrence, *Letters*, ed. James Boulton (Cambridge University Press, Cambridge, 1979), Vol. II, p. 183. See also Catherine Belsey, *Critical Practice* (Methuen, London, 1985), pp. 67–84; H. Stuart Hughes, *Consciousness and Society: The reorientation of European thought 1890–1930* (Harvester Wheatsheaf, Hemel Hempstead, 1979).

19. See John Batchelor, *The Edwardian Novelists* (Duckworth, London, 1982).

20. Edward Said, *Orientalism* (Vintage Books, New York, 1979).

21. See Ian Watt, *Conrad in the Nineteenth Century* (University of California Press, Berkeley, 1979).

22. Joseph Conrad, *Notes on Life and Letters* (Dent, London, 1970), p. 14.

23. Kenneth Ballhatchet, *Race, Sex and Class under the Raj* (Weidenfeld & Nicholson, London, 1980).

24. Fredric Jameson, *The Political Unconscious: Narrative as a socially symbolic act* (Cornell University Press, Ithaca, 1981), p. 207.

25. Conrad, *Notes on Life and Letters*, p. 89.
26. H. G. Wells, *The New Machiavelli* (Odhams, London, n.d.), Part I, Ch. 4.
27. Conrad, *Letters*, Vol. II, p. 228.
28. Kipling, *Kim* (Macmillan, London, 1919), Ch. 7.
29. A. R. JanMohammed, 'The economy of Manichean allegory: the function of racial difference in colonial literature', *Critical Inquiry*, Vol. 12 (1985) p. 78.
30. I. F. Clarke, *Voices Prophesying War 1763-1984* (Oxford University Press, London, 1966); Samuel Hynes, *The Edwardian Turn of Mind* (Princeton University Press, Princeton, 1968), pp. 33-53.
31. G. B. Shaw, *John Bull's Other Island* (Constable, London, 1936), p. 84.
32. See Martin Meisel, *Shaw and the Nineteenth-Century Theatre* (Princeton University Press, Princeton, 1963).
33. Shaw, *Collected Letters*, ed. Dan Laurence (Reinhardt, London, 1972), Vol. II, pp. 457-8.

CHAPTER 3

1. C. F. Masterman, *The Condition of England* (Methuen, London, 1911).
2. E. M. Forster, *Howards End* (Penguin, Harmondsworth, 1965), Ch. 5.
3. V. S. Naipaul, *An Area of Darkness* (Deutsch, London, 1964), pp. 207-10.
4. Feltes, pp. 76-98.
5. See Peter Widdowson, *E. M. Forster's Howards End: Fiction as history* (Chatto & Windus, London, 1977).
6. Hynes, *The Edwardian Turn of Mind*, pp. 127-32.
7. John Galsworthy, *Strife* (Duckworth, London, 1924), p. 74; p. 97.
8. Robert Tressell, *The Ragged Trousered Philanthropists* (Panther, London, 1975). See F. C. Ball, *One of the Damned: The life and times of Robert Tressell* (Weidenfeld & Nicholson, London, 1973); Peter Miles, 'The painters' Bible and the British workman: Robert Tressell's literary activity' in *The British*

Working-class Novel in the Twentieth Century, ed. Jeremy Hawthorn (Arnold, London, 1984), pp. 1–17; David Smith, *Socialist Propaganda in the English Novel* (Macmillan, London, 1978).

9. See Raymond Williams, 'The ragged arsed philanthropists', in his *Writing in Society* (Verso, London, n.d.), pp. 239–56.

10. Jack London, *The People of the Abyss* (Arco, London, 1963), Ch. 19.

11. Orwell, *Collected Essays*, Vol. I, p. 151. See also Tom Nairn, *The Break-up of Britain* (Verso, London, 1981), pp. 257–63.

12. Quiller-Couch, *Studies in Literature* (Cambridge University Press, Cambridge, 1918), p. 201.

13. Forster, *The Celestial Omnibus* (Sidgwick & Jackson, London, 1911).

14. Wells, *The War in the Air* (Penguin, Harmondsworth, 1973), Ch. 11.

15. Kipling, *A Diversity of Creatures* (Macmillan, London, 1917).

16. Lawrence, *The White Peacock* (Heinemann, London, 1960), Part II, Ch. 1.

17. Lawrence, *England my England* (Penguin, Harmondsworth, 1968), p. 32.

18. Wells, *Tono-Bungay* (Macmillan, London, 1911), Part I, Ch. 2.

19. M. J. Wiener, *English Culture and the Decline of the Industrial Spirit 1850–1980* (Penguin, Harmondsworth, 1987).

20. Tom Nairn, *The Enchanted Glass* (Radius, London, 1988), pp. 279–80.

21. See David Lodge, '*Tono-Bungay* and the condition of England', in his *Language of Fiction* (Routledge & Kegan Paul, London, 1966), pp. 214–42.

CHAPTER 4

1. Lawrence, *Letters*, Vol. I, p. 509.

2. Bennett, *Books and Persons*, pp. 88–100.

3. Bennett, *Clayhanger* (Penguin, Harmondsworth, 1976), Part I, Ch. 1.

4. Woolf, *The Captain's Deathbed*, p. 106.

5. See W. Bellamy, *The Novels of Wells, Bennett and Galsworthy 1890–1910* (Routledge & Kegan Paul, London, 1971).

6. Walter Pater, *The Renaissance* (Macmillan, London, 1912), p. 248.

7. Woolf, *Diaries*, ed. A. O. Bell (Hogarth Press, London, 1978), Vol. III, p. 208.

8. Sigmund Freud, *Complete Psychological Works*, ed. and trans. J. Strachey (Hogarth Press, London, 1971), Vol. XIII, p. 142.

9. Carl Schorske, *Fin de Siècle Vienna* (Weidenfeld & Nicholson, London, 1980), p. xxvi. See also Rosalind Coward, *Patriarchal Precedents* (Routledge & Kegan Paul, London, 1983).

10. J. M. Synge, *Collected Works*, ed. A. Price (Oxford University Press, London, 1966), Vol. II, p. 11.

11. Shaw, Preface to *Major Barbara* (Penguin, Harmondsworth, 1961), p. 23.

12. Raymond Williams, *The Long Revolution* (Chatto & Windus, London, 1961), p. 286.

13. Edmund Gosse, *Father and Son: A study of two temperaments* (Penguin, Harmondsworth, 1970), p. 5; p. 224.

14. Harley Granville Barker, *Collected Plays* (Sidgwick & Jackson, London, 1967), p. 178.

15. James Barrie, *Plays* (Hodder & Stoughton, London, 1933), p. 81.

16. Galsworthy, *The Forsyte Saga* (Penguin, Harmondsworth, 1980), Vol. I, Ch. 1.

17. Lawrence, *Selected Literary Criticism*, ed. Anthony Beal (Heinemann, London, 1969), p. 122; p. 125.

18. See Sheila Rowbotham and Jeffrey Weeks, *Socialism and the New Life: The personal and social politics of Edward Carpenter and Havelock Ellis* (Pluto, London, 1977).

19. Forster, *Maurice* (Arnold, London, 1971), p. 236.

20. *Maurice*, p. 240.

21. Lawrence, *Letters*, Vol. I, p. 459; Vol. I, p. 119; Vol. I, p. 453.

22. James Joyce, *A Portrait of the Artist* (Penguin, Harmondsworth, 1964), Ch. 5.

23. *Blast*, Vol. 1 (1914), p. 7.

CHAPTER 5

1. Elizabeth Robins, *The Convert* (Tauchnitz, Leipzig, 1908), Vol. II, Ch. 3.

2. See Gilbert and Gubar, *No Man's Land*, passim; Keating, *The Haunted Study*, pp. 175–96; Elaine Showalter, *A Literature of their Own* (Virago, London, 1984), pp. 216–39.

3. See Tess Cosslett, *Woman to Woman: Female friendship in fiction* (Harvester Wheatsheaf, Hemel Hempstead, 1988), pp. 138–82; Gail Cunningham, *The New Woman and the Victorian Novel* (Macmillan, London, 1978); Showalter, *A Literature of their Own*, pp. 182–215.

4. See Hynes, *The Edwardian Turn of Mind*, pp. 254–306; Keating, *The Haunted Study*, 241–85.

5. See Linda Dowling, 'The decadent and the New Woman in the 1890s', *Nineteenth Century Fiction*, Vol. 33 (1979), pp. 434–53.

6. See Hynes, *The Edwardian Turn of Mind*, pp. 22–33; Gareth Stedman-Jones, *Outcast London: A study in the relation between classes in Victorian society* (Clarendon Press, Oxford, 1971), pp. 322–36; Jeffrey Weeks, *Sex, Politics and Society: The regulation of sexuality since 1800* (Longman, London, 1981), pp. 122–40.

7. Anna Davin, 'Imperialism and motherhood', *History Workshop*, Vol. 5 (1978), pp. 9–65; G. R. Searle, *Eugenics and Politics in Britain 1900–1914* (Noordhoff, Leyden, 1976).

8. Wells, *A Modern Utopia* (Nelson, London, 1916), Ch. 6.

9. See Davin, 'Imperialism and motherhood'; Bernard Semmel, 'Karl Pearson', *British Journal of Sociology*, Vol. 9 (1958), pp. 111–25.

10. Charles Darwin, *The Descent of Man*, revised ed. (Murray, London, 1882), p. 599.

11. Wells, *Ann Veronica* (Penguin, Harmondsworth, 1968), Ch. 11.

12. Rebecca West, *The Strange Necessity* (Cape, London, 1928), pp. 199–200.

13. Weeks, *Sex, Politics and Society*, p. 126.

14. Shaw, *Man and Superman* (Penguin, Harmondsworth, 1976), p. 54.

15. Bennett, *Journals*, ed. Newton Flower (Cassell, London, 1932), Vol. I, p. 386.

16. Bennett, *Hilda Lessways* (Penguin, Harmondsworth, 1975), Part I, Ch. 4.

17. Lawrence, *Letters*, Vol. I, p. 459.

18. Shaw, *Our Theatre in the Nineties* (Constable, London, 1948), Vol. I, p. 75.

19. R. First and A. Scott, *Olive Schreiner* (Deutsch, London, 1980), pp. 266-7.
20. Olive Schreiner, *Woman and Labour* (Tauchnitz, Leipzig, 1911), p. 163; p. 153.
21. Julia Briggs, *A Woman of Passion: The life of E. Nesbit* (Hutchinson, London, 1987), p. 399.
22. Katherine Mansfield, *Collected Stories* (Constable, London, 1953), p. 742, p. 580.
23. Dorothy Richardson, *Pilgrimage* (Dent, London, 1938), Vol. I, p. 9.
24. May Sinclair, 'The novels of Dorothy Richardson', *The Egoist*, Vol. 5 (1918), p. 58.
25. Showalter, *A Literature of their Own*, p. 261.
26. John Rosenberg, *Dorothy Richardson, the Genius They Forgot: A critical biography* (Duckworth, London, 1973), p. 55.
27. Woolf, *Virginia Woolf: Women and writing*, ed. Michèle Barrett (Women's Press, London, 1988), p. 191.

CHAPTER 6

1. Hardy, *Life*, p. 444.
2. See Donald Davie, *Thomas Hardy and British Poetry* (Routledge & Kegan Paul, London, 1973), p. 73.
3. Lawrence, *Selected Literary Criticism*, p. 72.
4. Ford, *Critical Writings*, pp. 147-8.
5. See Doyle, *English and Englishness*.
6. Wells, *The New Machiavelli*, Part I, Ch. 4.
7. Orwell, *Critical Essays*, Vol. I, pp. 550-6.
8. Ford, *Critical Writings*, p. 148.
9. Ezra Pound, 'The later Yeats', in *Literary Essays of Ezra Pound*, ed. T. S. Eliot (Faber & Faber, London, 1954), pp. 378-81.
10. Hardy, *Life*, pp. 284-5.
11. Hardy, *Complete Poetical Works*, ed. Samuel Hynes (Clarendon Press, Oxford, 1984), Vol. I, p. 113.
12. Hardy, *Life*, p. 184.
13. Ford, *Critical Essays*, p. 36; pp. 41-2.
14. Hardy, *Life*, p. 384; p. 378.
15. See Henry Gifford, 'Hardy and Emma', *Essays and Studies*, Vol. 19 (1966) pp. 106-21; Tom Paulin, *Thomas Hardy: The poetry of perception* (Macmillan, London, 1986).

16. Hardy, *The Dynasts* (Macmillan, London, 1924), p. 454.
17. Ford, *Memories and Impressions*, p. 205–6.
18. Quiller-Couch, *Studies in Literature*, pp. 200–1.
19. F. R. Leavis, *New Bearings in English Poetry* (Chatto & Windus, London, 1950), p. 55.
20. Yeats, *Oxford Book of Modern Verse*, p. xiii.
21. Yeats, *Letters*, ed. A. Wade (Hart-Davis, London, 1954), p. 434.
22. T. S. Eliot, *Selected Prose*, ed. John Hayward (Penguin, Harmondsworth, 1965), p. 190.
23. Hardy, *Life*, p. 384; Hynes, *The Pattern of Hardy's Poetry* (Chapel Hill, North Carolina, 1956), p. 65.
24. See Norman Jeffares, *W. B. Yeats: Man and poet* (Routledge & Kegan Paul, London, 1962), pp. 128–9.
25. Yeats, *Letters*, p. 478.
26. Pound, *Literary Essays*, p. 378.
27. *Kipling: The critical heritage*, ed. R. L. Green (Routledge & Kegan Paul, London, 1971), p. 326.
28. T. E. Hulme, *Speculations*, ed. Herbert Read (Kegan Paul, Trubner & Trench, London, 1924), p. 118; p. 126.
29. See Frank Kermode, *Romantic Image* (Fontana, London, 1971); Michael Levenson, *A Genealogy of Modernism: A study of English literary doctrine 1908–1922* (Cambridge University Press, Cambridge, 1984).
30. Ford, *Critical Essays*, p. 54.
31. *Georgian Poetry 1911–1912*, ed. Edward Marsh (Poetry Bookshop, London, 1912).
32. Thomas, *A Language not to be Betrayed*, p. 112; p. 115.
33. Hardy, *Collected Letters*, ed. Richard Purdy and Michael Millgate (Clarendon Press, Oxford, 1988), Vol. VII, p. 113.
34. Woolf, *Collected Letters*, ed. N. Nicholson (Hogarth Press, London, 1971), Vol. II, p. 419.
35. Charlotte Mew, *Collected Poems and Prose*, ed. Val Warner (Carcanet/Virago, London, 1981), pp. 1–2.

CHAPTER 7

1. James, 'The New Novel', in *Selected Literary Criticism*, p. 361. Quotations throughout are from this version. 'The Younger

Generation' is reprinted in Edel and Ray, *Henry James and H. G. Wells*, pp. 178–214.

2. James, *Selected Criticism*, p. 287.
3. James, *The Art of the Novel*, p. 296.
4. James, *The Wings of the Dove* (Eyre & Spottiswoode, London, 1948), Ch. 5.
5. James, *The Ivory Tower* (Collins, London, 1917), p. 136; p. 301.
6. James, *The Notebooks*, ed. F. O. Matthiessen and K. B. Murdock (Oxford University Press, New York, 1961), p. 171.
7. Ian Watt, 'The first paragraph of *The Ambassadors*: an explication', *Essays in Criticism*, Vol. 10 (1960) pp. 250–74; Seymour Chatman, *The Later Style of Henry James* (Blackwell, Oxford, 1972).
8. Masterman, *The Condition of England*, pp. 49–50.
9. Edel and Ray, *Henry James and H. G. Wells*, p. 67; pp. 104–5; p. 111; p. 123; p. 127.
10. Edel and Ray, p. 103; p. 164. For Kipling reference see James, *Letters*, ed. Leon Edel (Harvard University Press, Cambridge, Mass., 1970) p. 70.
11. Edel and Ray, p. 130.
12. James, *The Art of the Novel*, p. 317; p. 321.
13. Edel and Ray, p. 128.
14. Edel and Ray, p. 121.
15. Wells, *Experiment in Autobiography* (Gollancz, London, 1934), Vol. II, pp. 494–5.
16. Lawrence, *Letters*, Vol. II, p. 183.
17. Edel and Ray, p. 261; p. 264; p. 245.
18. Wells, 'The discovery of the future', *Nature*, Vol. 65 (1902) pp. 326–31.
19. Wells, 'The contemporary novel', in Edel and Ray, p. 148.
20. Wells, *Boon*, quoted in Edel and Ray, p. 247.
21. Edel and Ray, p. 160.
22. Raymond Williams, *The English Novel from Dickens to Lawrence* (Paladin, St Albans, 1974), pp. 97–113.
23. Chatman, *The Later Style of Henry James*, p. 31.
24. Conrad, *The Nigger of the Narcissus* (Dent, London, 1960), pp. 3–5.
25. Conrad, *Notes on Life and Letters*, p. 84.
26. Conrad, *Notes on Life and Letters*, p. 13; p. 19.
27. Ford, *Joseph Conrad: A personal reminiscence* (Duckworth, London, 1924), p. 182.

28. Ernest Hemingway, *Byline: Hemingway*, ed. William White (Penguin, Harmondsworth, 1970), p. 135.
29. Ford, Preface to *The Good Soldier* (Penguin, Harmondsworth, 1976), p. 7.
30. Ford, *Critical Writings*, p. 43.
31. Ford, *Memories and Impressions*, pp. 343–57.
32. Lawrence, *Letters*, Vol. I. p. 165.
33. Joyce, *Letters*, ed. Richard Ellmann (Faber & Faber, London, 1966), Vol. II, p. 134.
34. Pound, *Literary Essays*, p. 399.
35. Joyce, *A Portrait of the Artist as a Young Man*, Ch. 5.
36. Woolf, The Common Reader (Hogarth Press, London, 1962), p. 187; *The Captain's Deathbed*, p. 104.
37. Woolf, *The Death of the Moth* (Readers' Union, London, 1943), p. 112.
38. West, *The Strange Necessity*, pp. 199–213.

Edwardian writers and books: a summary

This lists those writers mentioned in the text, and select works from that period. First publications are given as a reference point. Works mentioned in the text are asterisked. Dates given are those of first publication, except in the case of plays, where date of first performance is given instead.

Barrie, James Matthew (1860–1937) dramatist, novelist and children's writer. First novel: *Better Dead*, 1887. Works in this period include the plays, *Quality Street*, 1902; *The Admirable Crichton*, 1902; *Peter Pan, 1904; What Every Woman Knows*, 1908; and the children's books, *Peter Pan in Kensington Gardens*, 1906; *Peter and Wendy*, 1911.

Bennett, Enoch Arnold (1867–1931) novelist and critic. First novel: *A Man from the North*, 1898. His major Edwardian works are the Potteries novels, *Anna of the Five Towns, 1902; *The Old Wives' Tale, 1908; *Clayhanger, 1910, and its sequel, *Hilda Lessways*, 1911. Other works include the Potteries novels, *Whom God Hath Joined*, 1906, and *The Card*, 1911; the short story collection, *The Grim Smile of the Five Towns*, 1907; the thriller, *The Grand Babylon Hotel*, 1902. His regular column in the *New Age* was collected in *Books and Persons, 1917. See Letters*, ed. James Hepburn (Oxford University Press, London, 1966–86), 4 vols.; *Journals* ed. Newton Flower (Cassell, London, 1932–3), 3 vols.

Brooke, Rupert (1887–1915): poet. First book: *Poems*, 1911. Contributor to *Georgian Poetry 1911–1912*.

Burnett, Frances Hodgson (1849–1924) children's writer and novelist. First novel: *That Lass o' Lowrie's*, 1877. Works of this period include the children's books, *The Little Princess*, 1905; *The Secret Garden*, 1911.

Butler, Samuel (1835–1902) novelist and essayist. First novel: *Erewhon*, 1872. His posthumously published novel, *The Way of all Flesh*, written in the 1870s, was very influential in this period.

Carpenter, Edward (1844–1929) writer on socialism and sexuality. First book: *Towards Democracy*, 1883 (poem). Writings in this period include *The Art of Creation*, 1904, and *The Intermediate Sex*, 1908.

Chesterton, Gilbert Keith (1874–1936) essayist, novelist and poet. First book: *The Wild Knight*, 1900 (poems). Works of this period include the fantasy novels, *The Napoleon of Notting Hill*, 1904, and *The Man who was Thursday*, 1908; the collection of detective stories, *The Innocence of Father Brown*, 1911; the essays, *Heretics*, 1905, and *Orthodoxy*, 1908; the critical work, *The Victorian Age in Literature*, 1913.

Childers, Erskine (1870–1922) writer and politician. First book: *In the Ranks of the CIV*, 1900 (military memoirs). Wrote the influential spy thriller, *The Riddle of the Sands*, 1903.

Conrad, Joseph (born Josef Teodor Konrad Korzeniowski) (1857–1924) novelist and short-story writer, from Poland. First novel: *Almayer's Folly*, 1895. Major works of this period are the novels, *Lord Jim*, 1900; *Nostromo*, 1904; *The Secret Agent*, 1906; *Under Western Eyes*, 1911; and the novellas, *Heart of Darkness*, 1902; *Typhoon*, 1903. Other works include the novel *Chance*, 1913; the memoirs, *The Mirror of the Sea*, 1906, and *A Personal Record*, 1912; the short stories, 'Amy Foster' and 'Falk', collected in *Typhoon and other stories*, 1903, and 'The Secret Sharer', collected in *'Twixt Land and Sea*, 1912; the essays, *'Autocracy and War'* and *'Henry James'*, both 1905, collected in *Notes on Life and Letters*, 1921. See *Collected Letters*, ed. Frederick Karl and Laurence Davies (Cambridge University Press, Cambridge, 1983–8), 3 vols to date.

Corelli, Marie (born Mary Mackay) (1855-1924) best-selling novelist. First novel: *A Romance of Two Worlds*, 1886. Works of this period include *Temporal Power*, 1902; *The Treasure of Heaven*, 1906; *Woman or Suffragette?*, 1907.

Davies, William Henry (1871-1940) poet and autobiographer. First book: *The Soul's Destroyer and Other Poems*, 1905. Other works of the period include *The Autobiography of a Super-Tramp*, 1908, and contributions to *Georgian Poetry 1911-1912*, 1912.

De la Mare, Walter (1873-1956) poet and short-story writer. First book: *Songs of Childhood*, 1902. Works in this period include the poetry collection, *The Listeners*, 1912, and contributions to *Georgian Poetry 1911-1912*, 1912.

Doyle, Arthur Conan (1859-1930) short-story writer and novelist. First novel: *A Study in Scarlet*, 1887. Works in this period include *The Hound of the Baskervilles*, 1902; *The Return of Sherlock Holmes*, 1905; the science fiction novel, *The Lost World*, 1912.

Ford, Ford Madox (born Ford Herman Hueffer) (1873-1939) novelist and editor. First book: *The Brown Owl*, 1892 (fairy-story). Major work of the period was the novel, *The Good Soldier*, 1915. Other works include the historical *Fifth Queen* trilogy, 1907-8; two novels in collaboration with Conrad, *The Inheritors*, 1901, and *Romance*, 1903; the essays *'Impressionism – some Speculations'*, 1911, and *'On Impressionism'*, 1914, collected in *Critical Writings of Ford Madox Ford*, ed. Frank MacShane (University of Nebraska Press, Lincoln, 1964). Edited *The English Review*. Wrote several volumes of reminiscences of the period; a selection appears in *Memories and Impressions*, ed. Michael Killigrew (Penguin, Harmondsworth, 1979).

Forster, Edward Morgan (1879-1970) novelist, critic and short-story writer. First novel: *Where Angels Fear to Tread*, 1905. Works in this period include the novels, *The Longest Journey*, 1907; *A Room with a View*, 1908; *Howards End*, 1910; *Maurice*, unpublished until 1971. Also wrote much of *A Passage to India*, 1924, and the science fiction story, *'The Machine Stops'*, collected in *The Celestial Omnibus*, 1911.

Galsworthy, John (1867–1933): novelist and dramatist. First novel: *Jocelyn*, 1898. Major work of the period was *The Man of Property*, 1906, first novel in the *Forsyte Saga* sequence, of which the later volumes followed after World War I. Other works included the novel, *The Country House*, 1907, and the plays, *The Silver Box*, 1906, *Strife*, 1909, and *Justice*, 1910.

Gosse, Edmund (1849–1928) autobiographer and essayist. First book: *On Viol and Flute*, 1873 (verse). Major work of the period was the autobiographical *Father and Son*, 1907.

Grahame, Kenneth (1859–1932) children's writer and essayist. First book: *Pagan Papers*, 1893 (essays). Major work of the period was *The Wind in the Willows*, 1908.

Granville-Barker, Harley (1877–1946) dramatist, director, actor, critic. First play: *The Marrying of Ann Leete*, 1902. Other plays include *The Voysey Inheritance*, 1905; *Waste*, performance banned 1907; *The Madras House*, 1910. Directed and acted in Shaw's plays of the period, and directed plays by Galsworthy, and Hardy's *The Dynasts*.

Haggard, Henry Rider (1856–1925) novelist and writer on agricultural and imperial matters. First novel: *Dawn*, 1885. Works in this period include the novel, *Ayesha*, 1905, and the survey, *Rural England*, 1902.

Hardy, Thomas (1840–1928) poet and novelist. First novel: *Desperate Remedies*, 1871. Works in this period include the collections of poems, *Poems of the Past and the Present*, 1901; *Time's Laughingstocks*, 1909; *Satires of Circumstance*, which included *Poems of 1912–13*, 1914; the three-part verse drama, *The Dynasts*, 1904–8. See his autobiography dictated to his wife Florence Hardy, *The Life of Thomas Hardy*, (Macmillan, London, 1962); *Collected Letters*, ed. Richard Purdy and Michael Millgate (Clarendon Press, Oxford, 1978–88), 7 vols.; *The Literary Notebooks of Thomas Hardy*, ed. Lennart Bjork (Macmillan, London, 1985), 2 vols.

Hobson, John (1858–1940) writer on social and economic issues.

First book: *The Physiology of Industry*, 1889. Works in this period include **The Psychology of Jingoism*, 1901, and **Imperialism*, 1902.

Hulme, Thomas Ernest (1883–1917) essayist and poet. Major work of this period was the essay **'Romanticism and Classicism'*, 1912, collected in the posthumous first book, *Speculations*, ed. Herbert Read, 1924.

James, Henry (1843–1916) novelist, short-story writer and critic, from the United States. First novel: *Watch and Ward*, 1871. Major works of this period are the novels, **The Wings of the Dove*, 1902; **The Ambassadors*, 1903; **The Golden Bowl*, 1904. Other works include the short stories, 'The Beast in the Jungle', collected in *The Better Sort*, 1903; 'The Jolly Corner', collected in *The Altar of the Dead and other stories*, 1909; 'The Bench of Desolation', collected in *The Finer Grain*, 1910; the unfinished novels, *The Sense of the Past*, and **The Ivory Tower*, both 1917; the survey, *The American Scene*, 1906; critical essays, including **'The New Novel'*, 1914, collected in *Notes on Novelists*, 1914; the **Prefaces for the New York Edition of his works, 1906–10. See also his *Letters*, ed. Leon Edel (Harvard University Press, Cambridge, Mass., 1974–84), 4 vols.; *The Complete Notebooks*, ed. Leon Edel and Lyall Powers (Oxford University Press, Oxford, 1987); the correspondence with H. G. Wells collected in *Henry James and H. G. Wells*, ed. Leon Edel and Gordon Ray (Hart-Davis, London, 1958); the essays collected in *Selected Literary Criticism*, ed. Morris Shapira (Penguin, Harmondsworth, 1968); the Prefaces to the New York Edition collected in *The Art of the Novel*, ed. R. P. Blackmur (Scribner, New York, 1934).

Joyce, James Augustine Aloysius (1882–1941) novelist, short-story writer and poet. First book: *Chamber Music*, 1907 (poems). Works written in this period include the short story sequence, **Dubliners*, 1914, and the novel, **A Portrait of the Artist as a Young Man*, 1916. See also *Letters*, ed. Stuart Gilbert and Richard Ellmann (Faber & Faber, London, 1957–66), 3 vols.

Kipling, Rudyard (1865–1936): short-story writer, novelist and poet. First book: *Echoes*, 1885 (poems). Works in this period include the novel **Kim*, 1901; the short stories, 'Wireless', 'They', **Mrs Bathurst* and **'Below the Mill Dam'*, collected in

Traffics and Discoveries, 1904; *'An Habitation Enforced', collected in *Actions and Reactions*, 1909; *'As Easy as ABC', collected in *A Diversity of Creatures*, 1917; the children's books, *The Just So Stories*, 1902; **Puck of Pook's Hill*, 1906; **Rewards and Fairies*, 1910; the collection of poems, *The Five Nations, 1903.

Lawrence, David Herbert (1885–1930) novelist, short-story writer, poet, critic. First novel: **The White Peacock*, 1911. Work in this period includes the novels, *The Trespasser*, 1912, and *Sons and Lovers, 1913; much of the writing for *The Rainbow*, 1915, *Women in Love*, 1920, and *The Lost Girl, 1920; the short stories collected in **The Prussian Officer*, 1914; poems including contribution to **Georgian Poetry 1911–1912*, 1912. See also *Letters*, ed. James Boulton (Cambridge University Press, Cambridge, 1979–89), 5 vols.

London, Jack (1876–1916) novelist and journalist, from United States. Wrote the documentary study of Edwardian London, **The People of the Abyss*, 1903.

Mansfield, Katherine (born K. M. Beauchamp) (1888–1923) short-story writer, from New Zealand. First book: **In a German Pension*, 1912 (short stories). Other stories written in this period were published posthumously in **Something Childish and other stories*, 1924. See also *Collected Letters 1903–17*, ed. V. O'Sullivan and M. Scott (Clarendon Press, Oxford, 1984), 2 vols.

Masefield, John (1878–1967) poet and novelist. First book: *Salt-Water Ballads*, 1902. Other works include *Ballads and Poems*, 1910, and contributions to **Georgian Poetry 1911–1912*, 1912.

Masterman, Charles Frederick (1874–1927) writer on social matters and politician. First book: *Heart of the Empire*, 1900 (editor). Other writings in this period include *From the Abyss*, 1902; *In Peril of Change*, 1905; **The Condition of England*, 1909.

Mew, Charlotte (1869–1928) poet and short-story writer. First book: **The Farmer's Bride*, 1915, which collected her poems of the period.

Nesbit, Edith (1858–1924) children's writer and novelist. First novel: *The Prophet's Mantle*, 1886. Children's books in this period include *The Wouldbegoods*, 1901; *Five Children and It*, 1902; **The Amulet*, 1905; *The Railway Children*, 1906; *Harding's Luck*, 1909.

Orczy, Emmuska (1865–1947) best-selling novelist, from Hungary. First novel: *The Emperor's Candlesticks*, 1899. Works in this period include **The Scarlet Pimpernel*, 1905, based on her play of the same title, 1903. It was followed by *I Will Repay*, 1906, *The Elusive Pimpernel*, 1908, and other sequels.

Pound, Ezra (1885–1972) poet and critic, from the United States. First book: *A Lume Spirito*, 1908 (poems). Other works in the period include the collections of poems, *Personae*, 1909; *Canzoni*, 1911; *Ripostes*, 1912. He edited the anthology, **Des Imagistes*, 1914. His reviews of the period are collected in *Literary Essays*, ed. T. S. Eliot (Faber & Faber, London, 1954).

Quiller-Couch, Arthur (1863–1944) critic and novelist. First novel: *Dead Man's Rock*, 1887. Edited the **Oxford Book of English Verse*, 1900. His Cambridge lectures are collected in **Studies in Literature*, 1918, and **On the Art of Writing*, 1919.

Richardson, Dorothy Miller (1873–1957) novelist. First novel: **Pointed Roofs*, 1915. This was the first in her sequence of stream-of-consciousness novels, *Pilgrimage*, 1915–67.

Robins, Elizabeth (1862–1942) novelist, dramatist and actress, from the United States. First novel: *Alan's Wife*, 1893. Major work of the period was the novel, **The Convert*, 1907, based on her play, **Votes for Women*, 1907. (*The Convert* was republished by the Women's Press, 1980.)

Schreiner, Olive Emilie (1855–1920) novelist and writer on social matters, from South Africa. First novel: *The Story of an African Farm*, 1883. Major work of this period was **Woman and Labour*, 1910.

Shaw, George Bernard (1856–1950) dramatist, critic and socialist writer. First novel: *Cashel Byron's Profession*, 1886. Works in this period include the plays, **Man and Superman*, 1903; **John Bull's Other Island*, 1904; **Major Barbara*, 1905; *The Doctor's Dilemma*,

1906; *Getting Married*, 1908; *Misalliance*, 1910; *Pygmalion*, 1914; and the political pamphlet, **Fabianism and the Empire*, 1900. See also *Letters*, ed. Dan Laurence (Reinhardt, London, 1965–88), 3 vols.

Sinclair, May (1863–1946) novelist, critic and poet. First book: *Nakiketas and other poems*, 1887. Novels of the period include *The Divine Fire*, 1904; *The Creators*, 1910; *The Three Sisters*, 1914.

Synge, John Millington (1871–1909) dramatist. First play: *The Shadow of the Glen*, 1903. Other plays include *Riders to the Sea*, 1904; *The Well of the Saints*, 1905; **The Playboy of the Western World*, 1907; *The Tinker's Wedding*, 1909; *Deirdre of the Sorrows*, 1910.

Thomas, Philip Edward (1878–1917) poet, critic and writer on the countryside. First book: *The Woodland Life*, 1897. Works in this period include **The Heart of England*, 1906; **The South Country*, 1909. Began writing poetry in late 1914. For a selection of his reviews of writers of this period see *A Language not to be Betrayed: Selected prose of Edward Thomas*, ed. Edna Longley (Carcanet, Manchester, 1981).

Tressell, Robert (born Robert Noonan) (1870?–1911) novelist. His only novel, **The Ragged Trousered Philanthropists*, was posthumously published in abridged form in 1914. The full version was first published in 1955.

Wells, Herbert George (1866–1946) novelist, short-story writer and socialist writer. First novel: *The Time Machine*, 1895. Works in this period include the social novels, *Love and Mr Lewisham*, 1900; *Kipps*, 1905; **Tono-Bungay*, 1909; **Ann Veronica*, 1909; *The History of Mr Polly*, 1910; **The New Machiavelli*, 1911; the science-fiction novels, *The First Men in the Moon*, 1901; **The War in the Air*, 1908; the Utopian speculations, **Mankind in the Making*, 1903; **A Modern Utopia*, 1905; the critical essay **'The Contemporary Novel'*, 1911. See also *Experiment in Autobiography* (Gollancz, London, 1934), 2 vols.; *H. G. Wells's Literary Criticism*, ed. Patrick Parrinder and Robert Philmus (Harvester Wheatsheaf, Hemel Hempstead, 1980); *Henry James and H. G. Wells*, ed. Leon Edel and Gordon Ray, (Hart-Davis, London, 1958).

Woolf, Adeline Virginia (1882–1941) novelist and critic. First novel: *The Voyage Out*, 1915. Influential articles on this period are *'Modern Fiction', 1919, collected in *The Common Reader*, 1925, and *'Mr Bennett and Mrs Brown', 1924, collected in *The Captain's Deathbed*, 1950. See also *Collected Letters*, ed. N. Nicholson (Hogarth Press, London, 1971–80), 6 vols.

Yeats, William Butler (1865–1939) poet and dramatist. First book: *The Wanderings of Oisin and other poems*, 1889. Works of the period include the collections of poems, *In the Seven Woods*, 1904; *The Green Helmet and other poems*, 1910; *Responsibilities*, 1914; the plays *The King's Threshold*, 1903; *The Shadowy Waters*, 1904, *On Baile's Strand*, 1904; *Deirdre*, 1907. See *Letters*, ed. A. Wade (Hart-Davis, London, 1954).

Suggestions for further reading

GENERAL

For the history of the period see George Dangerfield, *The Strange Death of Liberal England* (Constable, London, 1935); Eric Hobsbawm, *The Age of Empire 1875–1914* (Weidenfeld & Nicholson, London, 1987); *The Invention of Tradition*, ed. Eric Hobsbawm and Terence Ranger (Cambridge University Press, Cambridge, 1983); Donald Read, *Edwardian England, 1901–1915: Society and Politics* (Harrap, London, 1972), and *Documents from Edwardian England, 1901–1915* (Harrap, London, 1973).

For cultural history see H. Stuart Hughes, *Consciousness and Society: The reorientation of European social thought 1890–1930* (MacGibbon & Kee, London, 1959); Samuel Hynes, *The Edwardian Turn of Mind* (Princeton University Press, Princeton, 1968); Stephen Kern, *The Culture of Time and Space 1880–1918* (Weidenfeld & Nicholson, London, 1983); Raymond Williams, *Culture and Society 1780–1950* (Chatto & Windus, London, 1958), pp. 166–99.

For the literary history of the period see John Batchelor, *The Edwardian Novelists* (Duckworth, London, 1982); Samuel Hynes, *Edwardian Occasions: Essays on English writing in the early twentieth century* (Routledge & Kegan Paul, London, 1972); Peter Keating, *The Haunted Study: A social history of the English novel 1875–1914* (Secker & Warburg, London, 1989); Hugh Kenner, *A Sinking Island* (Barrie & Jenkins, London, 1988); Frank Kermode, 'The

English Novel *c.* 1907', in his *Essays on Fiction 1971–82* (Routledge & Kegan Paul, London, 1983), pp. 33–51; John Lester, *Journey through Despair: Transformations in British literary culture 1880–1914* (Princeton University Press, Princeton, 1968).

For changes in status of author and text see Chris Baldick, *The Social Mission of English Criticism 1848–1932* (Clarendon Press, Oxford, 1983); Brian Doyle, *English and Englishness* (Routledge, London, 1989); N. N. Feltes, *Modes of Production of Victorian Novels* (Chicago University Press, Chicago, 1983); Terry Lovell, *Consuming Fiction* (Verso, London, 1987). For popular fiction see Richard Altick, *The English Common Reader: A social history of the mass reading public 1800–1900* (Chicago University Press, Chicago, 1957) for the period immediately before; Claud Cockburn, *Bestseller: The books that everyone read 1900–1959* (Sidgwick & Jackson, London, 1972), Q. D. Leavis, *Fiction and the Reading Public* (Chatto & Windus, London, 1939), pp. 205–74.

CHAPTER 2

For attitudes to race and empire see Kenneth Ballhatchet, *Race, Sex and Class under the British Raj* (Weidenfeld & Nicholson, London, 1980); Christine Bolt, *Victorian Attitudes to Race* (Routledge & Kegan Paul, 1971); V. G. Kiernan, *The Lords of Human Kind: European attitudes to the outside world in the imperial age* (Weidenfeld & Nicholson, London, 1969); Edward Said, *Orientalism* (Pantheon, New York, 1978); Lewis Wurgaft, *The Imperial Imagination: Magic and myth in Kipling's India* (Wesleyan University Press, Middletown, 1983).

For studies of the literature of empire see Patrick Brantlinger, *The Rule of Darkness: British literature and imperialism 1830–1914* (Cornell University Press, Ithaca, 1988); Joanna de Groot, ' "Sex" and "Race": The construction of language and image in the nineteenth century', in *Sexuality and Subordination: Studies of gender in the nineteenth century*, ed. Susan Mendus and Jane Rendall (Routledge, London, 1989), pp. 89–128; Martin Green, *Dreams of Adventure, Deeds of Empire* (Basic books, New York, 1979); Louis James, 'Tom Brown's imperialist sons', *Victorian Studies*, Vol. 17 (1973) pp. 89–99; A. R. Jan Mohammed, 'The economy of Manichean allegory: The function of racial difference in colonial literature', *Critical*

Inquiry, Vol. 12 (1985) pp. 59–87; *Imperialism and Popular Culture*, ed. John Mackenzie (Manchester University, Manchester, 1986); *Imperialism and Juvenile Literature*, ed. Jeffrey Richards (Manchester University Press, Manchester, 1989); Alan Sandison, *The Wheel of Empire: A study of the imperial idea in some late nineteenth-century and early twentieth-century fiction* (Macmillan, London, 1967); Brian Street, *The Savage in Literature: Representations of 'primitive' society in English fiction 1858–1920* (Routledge & Kegan Paul, London, 1975).

On Conrad see Avrom Fleischman, *Conrad's Politics: Community and anarchy in the fiction of Joseph Conrad* (Johns Hopkins Press, Baltimore, 1967); Fredric Jameson, *The Political Unconscious: Narrative as a socially symbolic act* (Cornell University Press, Ithaca, 1981); Benita Parry, *Conrad and Imperialism* (Macmillan, London, 1983); Ian Watt, *Conrad in the Nineteenth Century* (University of California Press, Berkeley, 1979).

On Kipling see *Rudyard Kipling* and *Rudyard Kipling's Kim*, both ed. Harold Bloom, (Chelsea House, New York, 1987); John McClure, *Kipling and Conrad: The colonial fictions* (Harvard University Press, Cambridge, Mass., 1981); *Kipling's Mind and Art*, ed. Andrew Rutherford (Oliver & Boyd, Edinburgh, 1964); J. M. Tompkins, *The Art of Rudyard Kipling* (Methuen, London, 1959).

On Shaw see Martin Meisel, *Shaw and the Nineteenth-Century Theatre* (Princeton University Press, Princeton, 1963).

On spy fiction see David Stafford, 'Spies and Gentlemen: the Birth of the British Spy Novel 1893–1914', *Victorian Studies*, Vol. 24 (1981), pp. 489–509.

CHAPTER 3

On Englishness see *Englishness: Politics and culture 1880–1920*, ed. Robert Colls and Philip Dodd (Croom Helm, London, 1986); Tom Nairn, *The Break-Up of Britain* (New Left Books, London, 1977), and *The Enchanted Glass: Britain and its monarchy* (Radius, London, 1988); Martin Wiener, *English Culture and the Decline of the Industrial Spirit 1850–1980* (Cambridge University Press, Cambridge, 1981); Raymond Williams, *The Country and the City* (Chatto & Windus, London, 1973).

On Forster see Frederick Crews, *E. M. Forster: The perils of humanism* (Princeton University Press, Princeton, 1962); Peter

Widdowson, E. M. *Forster's Howards End: Fiction as history* (Chatto & Windus, London, 1977).
On Tressell see F. C. Ball, *One of the Damned: The life and times of Robert Tressell* (Weidenfeld & Nicholson, London, 1973); Peter Miles, 'The painters' Bible and the British workman', in *The British Working-class Novel in the Twentieth Century*, ed. Jeremy Hawthorn (Arnold, London, 1984), pp. 1–17; David Smith, *Socialist Propaganda in the English Novel* (Macmillan, London, 1978); Raymond Williams, 'The ragged arsed philanthropists', in his *Writing in Society* (Verso, London, n.d.).
On Wells see David Lodge, '*Tono-Bungay* and the Condition of England', in his *Language of Fiction* (Routledge and Kegan Paul, London, 1966).

CHAPTER 4

On parricide see Sigmund Freud, *Totem and Taboo* in *Complete Psychological Works*, ed. J. Strachey (Hogarth Press, London, 1971); also Rosalind Coward, *Patriarchal Precedents* (Routledge & Kegan Paul, London, 1983); Carl Schorske, 'Politics and patricide in Freud's *Interpretation of Dreams*', in his *Fin de Siècle Vienna* (Weidenfeld & Nicholson, London, 1980), pp. 181–207.
On Bennett see William Bellamy, *The Novels of Wells, Bennett and Galsworthy 1890–1910* (Routledge & Kegan Paul, London, 1971); John Lucas, *Arnold Bennett: A study of his fiction* (Methuen, London, 1974).
On the literary revolts of the period see Raymond Williams, *The Long Revolution* (Chatto & Windus, London, 1961), pp. 274–99; also see general section above.

CHAPTER 5

On women and empire see Anna Davin, 'Imperialism and motherhood', *History Workshop*, Vol. 5 (1978) pp. 9–65; Jane Mackay and Pat Thane, 'The Englishwoman', in *Englishness*, ed. Colls and Dodd, pp. 191–229. On the feminist movement see Olive Banks, *Faces of Feminism: A study of feminism as a social movement* (Blackwell,

Oxford, 1981); Richard J. Evans, *The Feminists: Women's emancipation movements in Europe, America and Australasia 1840-1920* (Croom Helm, London, 1977); Brian Harrison, *Separate Spheres: The opposition to women's suffrage* (Croom Helm, London, 1978).

On women's writing in the period see Linda Dowling, 'The decadent and the New Woman in the 1890s', *Nineteenth Century Fiction*, Vol. 33 (1979) pp. 434-53; Sandra Gilbert and Susan Gubar, *No Man's Land: The place of the woman writer in the twentieth century*, Vol. I, *The War of the Words*, and Vol. II, *Sexchanges* (Yale University Press, New Haven, 1988-9); Elaine Showalter, *A Literature of their Own: British women novelists from Brontë to Lessing* (Princeton University Press, Princeton, 1977); Patricia Stubbs, *Women and Fiction: Feminism and the novel 1880-1920* (Harvester Wheatsheaf, Hemel Hempstead, 1979).

On Mansfield see Kate Fullbrook, *Katherine Mansfield* (Harvester Wheatsheaf, Hemel Hempstead, 1986). On Richardson see Stephen Heath, 'Writing for Silence: Dorothy Richardson and the novel', in *Teaching the Text*, ed. Suzanne Kappeler and Norman Bryson (Routledge & Kegan Paul, London, 1983), pp. 126-47. On *The Voyage Out* see Gillian Beer, 'Virginia Woolf and prehistory', in her *Arguing with the Past* (Routledge & Kegan Paul, London, 1989); Louise de Salvo, *Virginia Woolf's First Voyage: A novel in the making* (Macmillan, London, 1980).

CHAPTER 6

For poetic directions in the period see F. R. Leavis, *New Bearings in English Poetry* (Chatto & Windus, London, 1950), pp. 27-75; John Lucas, *Modern English Poetry from Hardy to Hughes* (Batsford, London, 1986), pp. 50-69; John Press, *A Map of Modern English Verse* (Oxford University Press, London, 1969), pp. 30-52 and 105-31; C. K. Stead, *The New Poetic* (Hutchinson, London, 1964).

On Hardy see Donald Davie, *Thomas Hardy and British Poetry* (Routledge & Kegan Paul, London, 1973); Samuel Hynes, *The Pattern of Hardy's Poetry* (Chapel Hill, North Carolina, 1956); F. R. Leavis, *The Living Principle: English as a discipline of thought* (Chatto & Windus, London, 1975), pp. 127-54; Tom Paulin, *Thomas Hardy: The poetry of perception* (Macmillan, London, 1986, revised ed.).

On Yeats see Harold Bloom, *Yeats* (Oxford University Press, London, 1970); Richard Ellmann, *Yeats: The man and the masks* (Macmillan, London, 1949), and *The Identity of Yeats* (Faber & Faber, London, 1954); Norman Jeffares, *W. B. Yeats: Man and Poet* (Routledge & Kegan Paul, London, 1961, revised ed.).

On the antecedents of modernism see Frank Kermode, *Romantic Image* (Routledge & Kegan Paul, London, 1957); Michael Levenson, *A Genealogy of Modernism: A study of English literary doctrine 1908–1922* (Cambridge University Press, Cambridge, 1984). On the Georgians see Robert Ross, *The Georgian Revolt: Rise and fall of a poetic ideal* (Faber & Faber, London, 1967).

CHAPTER 7

On the literary debates of the period see the writers' letters, etc. listed in the Writers' Summary above. See also Linda Anderson, *Bennett, Wells and Conrad: Narrative in transition* (Macmillan, Basingstoke, 1988); N. Delbanco, *Group Portrait: Conrad, Crane, Ford, James and Wells* (Faber & Faber, London, 1982); Raymond Williams, *The English Novel from Dickens to Lawrence* (Chatto & Windus, London, 1970).

On James see Peter Brooks, *The Melodramatic Imagination* (Yale University Press, New Haven, 1976); Seymour Chatman, *The Later Style of Henry James* (Blackwell, Oxford, 1972); John Goode, 'The pervasive mystery of style: *The Wings of the Dove*', in his *The Air of Reality* (Methuen, London, 1972), pp.244–300; Ian Watt, 'The first paragraph of *The Ambassadors*: An explication', *Essays in Criticism*, Vol. 10 (1960) pp. 250–274.

On Wells see Linda Anderson, 'Self and society in Wells's *Tono-Bungay*', *Modern Fiction Studies*, Vol. 26 (1980) pp. 199–212; John Batchelor, *H. G. Wells* (Cambridge University Press, Cambridge, 1985).

On Ford see Frank Kermode, *Essays in Fiction*, pp. 96–101.

Index